To BarBara,
So Nice to meet you & cant wait
To see you again.
May God Bless your Journey!

~ Helen Ol Wheely

Printed in the U.S.A. by KDP

What Doesn't Kill You
Authored by Helen On Wheelz
Photographs provided by Helen On Wheelz

ISBN: 978-1-08-221507-0
Independently published
Biography & Autobiography

After her mother's untimely death when she was two years old, Helen On Wheelz was raised in Wisconsin by her older sister. From that day on, her life started to crumble. Helen's telling memoir *What Doesn't Kill You*, walks her readers through her shocking life of physical abuse, dysfunction, and neglect. But Helen is relentless. She finds *salvation* through opening her heart to The Lord, and now takes pride in telling others that they can find it, too. Today Helen enjoys contentment, serenity, and happiness. She is presently an over-the-road trucker and shares her trucking experience with her cat named *Animal*.

INTRODUCTION

I want to let you know that I am NOT a professional writer, nor do I have the delusion of thinking I am. What I know best are my own life experiences. Professional writers have informed me that my writing is not polished and that it is far from flowing properly. With great concern, I tried going the "professional route," and after all the time and money spent, I can honestly say that it is not right for this book. I'm still glad that I tried it, because it was part of the process of giving me the courage to complete my WHOLE story, which I would not have otherwise done.

So… time and money was not wasted, but was just what I needed. So, with that being said, I am not allowing this book to be altered other than some basic edits of grammar and punctuation. This is all my writing. The way the Good Lord has put it on my heart, I say this with great emotion because my flesh does not like this book-writing at all. To be totally exposed to everyone in the world is not a comforting thought. But, when I think about it, this book is REALLY NOT my book—it's God's—and I am only being totally obedient to His will by exposing my whole life story.

I know that this is my calling; I was chosen to do this. There is NO doubt in my mind. But the flesh is weak, so I must stay covered and focused on pushing through to the end. I plan to complete His will—at all costs. No dating, no long periods of time spent with others (including family and friends), until this book is released.

He wants me all to Himself, and I need to be okay with this… and I am.

In saying this, you the Readers, are my only concern. This is a self-help book, but there are some very traumatic experiences told. If you have never dealt with childhood trauma yourself, you may want to pass it along to someone who has. My heart's desire is to bring real peace and understanding to those who need and want it. I do not wish to anger, upset, or cause confusion to anyone. Drama is not my friend, and I will not play in its midst.

The world is full of "naysayers." This book is NOT for them.

PREVIEW

I am writing this book because there are many people who don't believe that there is a light at the end of the tunnel. Not only do I want to show you how I found it, but I also want to share my journey with you. This is a book about my life: The good, the bad, and the ugly, and how I got through it. I will share my heart and soul, the nuts and bolts of how I became FREE of the guilt and shame of it all. I will hold nothing back. You will soon know more about me than you probably know right now about yourself.

You may be asking, "Why?" "Why would you want to expose yourself like this?"

The answer is simple: Because NO ONE can hurt me anymore. NO ONE can hurt me—unless I choose to let them! It is that simple, and I will show you how I did it.

This is NOT a book for people who want to stay in their trauma-filled lives. Let me repeat myself…. This is NOT a book for those who want to stay the same. This book is for those who want OUT! This is for people who KNOW that they are in a place where they do NOT belong. It is for people who want more out of life.

There is more in life.
You know it.
You feel it.
You want it.

Maybe you don't know how to get it. YOU are the one I am writing this book for. It is dedicated to YOU. There are no simple solutions. It will take you time and hard work to better yourself—just as it is with anything in life. This is no exception.

I will walk you through all the steps and stages I went through to get where I am today. You will see the dysfunctional home I was raised in. From incest, to living with a child molester, the pain, torture, and sickness I was forced to endure for years.

The Loneliness
The Anger
The Guilt
The Betrayal
The Helplessness
The Self- Destruction.
ALL THE THINGS WE HATE TO TALK ABOUT.
To expose the sickness or cancer is always the first step in healing.

If you are not ready to deal with your situation, then again, this book is not for you… yet.

iv

Mind you, this is NOT a negative book. I am going to show you how to make lemonade out of lemons. I will show you how I went from:

VICTIM TO SURVIVOR
and...
SURVIVOR TO WARRIOR

Step by step, you will see how I dealt with suicide as well as the devil trying to take me out. You will read about the little child I was afraid of, and where I found her. You will see the anger that controlled me, and now I control.

This is a self-help book, but you must be ready to help yourself.
Are you... ?

As you turn the pages, some of you will realize that you are not alone. Some of you may think, "Well, I was never molested, how can this book help me?" This book is for any type of dysfunctional past—any kind of abuse. Do you have crutches or addictions such as smoking, drugs, or pornography? In other words, are you self-mutilating?

You may have lived with an alcoholic parent. You might have been physically or mentally abused as a child. Are you gay or transgender? Were you bullied in school? Do you have temper tantrums or anger issues? Are you out of control and don't know why? Do your actions scare you? Do you want to know why? Do you want answers?

My goal, hope and prayer is that, by telling my story, my journey, YOU may find hope and peace in your own life.

I started writing at about age 12, and I am now 53 years old. I sought professional help at age 22 and learned one thing through my walk: I never stop learning and growing. I stop when I take my final breath—and so do you.

Walk with me as I show you how I went from Victim to Survivor to Warrior, and I stopped letting my past control... MY future.

TABLE OF CONTENTS

1

MY ARRIVAL

I am the youngest of eight.

This is MY REAL life story. I will be exposing some things that some people will not appreciate. These are things I experienced in MY life. I saw them through MY eyes, and I remember them very vividly—even to this day.

What family members may think of this book is NOT my concern. My concern is to provide help for others who need help getting through similar situations in their own lives. I am here for you, the reader, to show you how I climbed a mountain that looked unreachable. It's not. But... you must be ready to invest in yourself, because that is what it takes to win at this life-long journey.

I was born in 1966 in Wisconsin. I was the youngest of eight living children. My mother also had given birth to two babies that didn't make it. So, all in all, my mother was pregnant for about 90 months before she died at age 39.

I really don't remember anything about her. I was told that she was a very strict woman with a lot of superstitions. She was a Catholic, as you can tell from the amount of children she had. She liked to smoke Pall Mall cigarettes and was a very proud woman. She took pride in how well behaved her children were. She was a very hard-working woman. I was told by one of the youngest of my sisters that I have my mother's demeanor. In other words, don't tell me I can't do something because I will gladly prove you wrong!

My father adopted my two oldest sisters when he married our mother. So, my two oldest sisters are actually my half-sisters. My mother and father went on to have three more girls, and three boys. I am the very youngest of the eight—by five years.

Right about the time I was born, my mother and father were not getting along very well. Apparently, my mother had found out that our father was cheating on her. He had a younger woman *on the side* who was also married. Many men stray although, they don't usually leave the woman they marry.

My father, I believe, was going through his change of life (no excuse), and left my mother and all his children. I don't believe that he knew of her illness at the time he left her. I am not here to judge him, either. We all make our own beds that we must lie in.

Oh, by the way, my mother's name was Helen—just like mine. My oldest brother was the boy who was named after our father.

There are a lot of things that happened to my mother as a child that were pretty horrible that were mostly brought on by her mother—my grandmother. I will tell you, my grandmother was a very money-hungry woman. Let's just say this… in my grandmother's mind, there was a price for EVERYTHING, and I mean everything.

This is a serious sign of weakness, in my world. My grandmother was a driven entrepreneur and had started many businesses in her lifetime. I have too, but the difference is that I have morals and standards that I live by. There are certain things that I will NOT do for money… no matter how much.

We lived in a house near a school. My father was a High Pressure Boiler Engineer there, and my mother worked in a factory. Two years after I was born, my mother passed away at the very young age of 39. She had gotten blood poisoning from the factory where she worked. Her fingers were literally rotting off her hands from the chemical damage they had suffered. I can only imagine the pain she must have been in during this time. Her doctor told her that she had about six months to live when he diagnosed her issue, but she didn't make it that long. *(I have always thought that after ten kids and almost 90 months of pregnancy, I would have died, too.)*

At the time of my mother's death, my oldest sister was 22 years of age—she's 20 years older than I. So… here we all were, our mother had just passed away and our father was off with some young woman, starting a new life for himself. Here was our oldest sister, 22 years old, in the prime of her life, with a house full of kids who needed to be raised. She had to take the reins because our second-oldest sister was already off to college.

Wow. Writing this all down on paper really makes me look at everything in a different light. I can see the hesitation of wanting to take this all on, as well as I can feel her need to want to run away from it all. This was not her fault… all these kids, plus one of her own who I called "Dudie." So much responsibility went along with it. My sister had her whole life ahead of her. Dreams to follow, places to see, things to do. Then... STOP! Now you're responsible for all these hungry mouths to feed that you didn't even bring into the world.

Now that I am writing this, I truly understand the anger she has had toward our father all this time. Right now, I truly get it. She felt obligated to raise all of us kids because we are, after all, her brothers and sisters. While my father was off flying like a free bird, trying his new wings, she was there for us.

My father was seven years older than our mother, so that made him about 46 years at our mother's death. I do remember his visiting us when we were growing up. I also remember my oldest sister not being friendly to him. I never understood that, but I see it very clearly now. Growing up, I never really got to know my father. I was very young when my mom was around, and the few times I saw him just seem like a blur to me. He seemed like a nice enough man, but there was no real closeness. I knew, growing up, "who" he was, but when he actually came to visit, it was always so brief. His visits were so few that it made it hard to bond with him.

I found out just a few weeks ago that our father did try many times to come to see us kids, but my sister hindered those visits. Apparently, when dad did try to come to see us, he was asked to call ahead. When he would call ahead, none of us kids would be home for him to see. Only my sister would be there waiting for him. My father would show up—expecting to see us kids—and we would not be home. Two of my sisters would sometimes come to visit with him. One of my sisters recalls going to the house for a visit, and none of us were there. When asked, "Where are the kids?" her response would be, "They had plans with their friends and I can't make them stay here if they don't want to." My sister told me that this happened many times. I couldn't help but think, "Where could I have been when my father came to visit me, because I was always home, it seemed." I really don't remember Dad coming to see us that often.

Then it hit me. Every so often, out of the blue, my sister would ask me what I was doing that weekend. I would think to myself, "I will be doing what I always do almost every weekend. I will be upstairs rotting in my bedroom." What a funny question, I would think. She would then say, "Why don't you go to your friend, Karen's, house this weekend?" I now remember that I said, "Wow, that would be great. Can I?" And my sister would say, "Why don't you give her a call and see if it's okay with her parents?" At first I thought, "Wow, that's cool. There is a party this weekend." Then, my thought would be, "What the heck is wrong with her? She never lets me go anywhere!" I remember telling Karen how weird she had been acting. How I never got to go to her house, and now my sister wants me to see if I can spend the night. I wasn't going to complain. I was just happy to get out of the house for once.

Now that I am an adult looking back on all this, I see what she was up to. It was those times that I was able to spend the night at my friend Karen's house—the times that my father was expected to come over and see us kids. I am 43 years old, and just figuring this out.

I don't know what she was trying to do by keeping us from seeing our own father, but when I stop and think about it: no time spent with our father meant no relationship with him, right?

I don't think the way she does, so it's hard for me to understand this conniving thought process. I can't help thinking about how all our darkness will be exposed by the light some day. For many of you who don't think so… the devil is alive and well.

To believe it, just stop and watch people when money is involved. And, don't think for one second that money is not involved in this story somehow. The love for money will always show a person's true colors.

Before I continue about money... let me sum up the story of my arrival. So... I grew up being raised by my older sister, hardly knowing my father, and not remembering my mother at all.

How is that for the start in life's journey?

2

MONEY

"It's easier for a camel to fit through the eye of a needle, than a rich man to enter the Kingdom of Heaven."

My oldest sister (should I say) has a thing with money like my grandma, and believe me, she has always been paid dearly for raising us kids. She actually told me once that she didn't want us kids because she was in the prime of her life. She ran away from the house and ended up calling her lawyer friend. He was the one who talked her into raising us.

He told her that she could become unbelievably wealthy if she did. Well, you know that's all she needed to hear before being "all in!" Not to mention the fact that she was protected by her big-shot lawyer friend—and she really was untouchable! He knew every little money loophole of the system, ranging from child support, trust funds, and suing the company that caused our mom's death. He even taught her where to hide the money.

I did say trust funds, didn't I? Yes, the monies from suing the company that caused mom's death went into trust funds for my three brothers and I to have once we turned of age. Her lawyer taught her how to drain all that legally through the courts, so by the time we each turned 18, it was all gone. We got nothing.

"Guilty?—Why should I feel guilty," she told me. "You kids took the best years of my life from me. YOU OWE ME for raising you!"

You know what? I call it blood money, and she can have it.

Mark 10:25
"It's easier for a camel to fit through the eye of a needle, than a rich man to enter the Kingdom of Heaven."

Then, there is the story of "Where is Mom?" Our mother was buried in a cemetery almost 50 years ago, but if you try to find her today, you won't. Someone else is there. Someone decided to exhume her body after all these years without any of the other siblings' knowledge or permission.

Who would do such a thing? Well, I'll give you one guess! Again, blood money, and I want no part of it. She can take that one to the grave with her because she is right when she says that *she is not like us.*

One of my full-blooded sisters went to visit Mom's grave and could not find her. She knew where she was buried, at least supposed to be, but someone else was there instead. My sister started crying, got back in her car, and drove up to the cemetery office to ask, "What happened to my mother's burial site?" Apparently, one of our siblings claimed that there were no living relatives and had her grave dug up and sold the plot to another family.

REALLY? WHO DOES THAT?

I can't imagine the shock and emptiness one may feel after expecting to see your own mom's name on the gravestone (where it had been for 40 plus years), and finding her missing and then replaced by someone else. I can only guess what would drive a person to do such a thing.

It's a powerful thing and controls many people today—as you can see. These people are morally and ethically weak in my book. And yes, THIS IS MY BOOK.

Oh, there is more, but I am already bored with this topic. My only question today, truly is... WHERE IS MOM?

3

MORALS

Why not treasure something that I can hold on to eternally?

I remember my father had given me a necklace once when I was a little girl. It looked like a garnet *(my birthstone—yes, I'm a Capricorn)* with diamonds around it. I treasured this dearly and still have it today.

I remember my sister invited some kids over to the house for a weekend. I guess she must have been baby-sitting for a friend from work. There were two boys and one girl. I really don't recall their names. I only remember showing the girl my jewelry box and all my jewelry. I did have some nice jewelry, and because my skin is hypo allergenic, it had to be real gold or silver or I would break out in a rash.

Anyway, I showed this girl the necklace that my father had given me and told her how very much it meant to me because I hardly ever saw him. The next day, she was packing her bag to leave, and as she was moving things around, I saw my necklace and some of my other things in her suitcase. I was shocked, but actually more pissed off than anything. I ran downstairs and told my sister who I called "Mom" about it. I said, "I saw some of my things in her suitcase!" She asked, "Are you sure?" I said, "Yes, and one of them was the necklace Dad gave me!" My sister called her down and told her to go get her bag and bring it downstairs. When the girl finally opened it up, underneath her socks was all my stuff—including my necklace.

From this day on, I have never liked thieves. I know what it feels like to have something you treasure dearly taken from you. It meant nothing to her, but she wanted what I had. This type of person saddens me. Back then, as a 12–year old girl, I wanted to punch her in the face for betraying me. Writing this today, I see an unhappy little girl who was visiting me. Now my thoughts are different. If you think my necklace will bring you any kind of happiness, I will give it to you. I do not value materialistic things like I used to and even though my earthly father is gone and that is the only gift I have from him in my possession, I can say that I would still give it to her.

It's not because I don't miss my earthly father. It's not because I don't treasure his meaning in my life. It's just because it is an earthly thing. All earthly things will someday go away and all we will have left is each other's presence of spirit and memories.

So… my thought is this: Why not treasure something that I can hold on to eternally… and not something that is only worldly?

4

DERAILED IN KINDERGARTEN

My heart starts beating louder.

My sister started taking Dudie and I to the park. We would run around and play, and a man would come by and sit by my sister on the park bench. Who is this man? I wondered. We started going to the park more and more and every time the same man would show up, and sit beside her and talk. One time I saw them kiss. *Oh no,* I am confused because she is married to Roger and he lives in our house. I say nothing, but know something is wrong. She tells us this man is her friend but I know better, even though I am only four or five years of age.

Then one day He shows up at our house and he and Roger are talking like best friends, laughing & drinking beer. I find out that he works at the same place Roger does. I still do not understand why he would kiss my sister (who I called mom).

As time goes on our house starts to get very scary. Roger and mom would be up night after night screaming and yelling and throwing things. I remember being in my room crying, just wanting to sleep. Covering my ears did not help because they were screaming at the top of their lungs. My life is falling apart, no warm fuzzies here–just horrible sounds echoing through the house... my safe place. Then one day the man starts sleeping over at our house, upstairs with us kids. I had my own room and Dudie and my brothers shared the largest room/half the upstairs. There was another room that connected to my room behind the staircase.

That is where that man was sleeping. In the middle of the night I hear a noise of soft, quiet, slow, footsteps. The sound starts to get louder and louder. My body freezes as I am scared out of my ever–loving mind wondering *who is entering my room?* I then see a flashlight streak across the floor it is coming from behind the staircase where there was an opening to my room. I am so scared, my heart starts beating louder and louder as it starts echoing in my ears. *It's that man!*

What could he possibly want in my room in the middle of the night? I lay still and frozen from fright and confusion. He then bends down near the middle of my bed and lifts my covers. I then feel my nightgown being lifted up towards my head as he pulls my underwear to the side. He licked me. I am really confused not understanding what he is doing or why. I am only in kindergarten and my innocence has just been derailed.

A few weeks later, Roger is gone and this man is now sleeping in my sisters bedroom.

I am going to tell you, I suffered him molesting me for years. Exactly how many I do not know. My guess is six or seven. This is not something we keep track of. Most of us try to bury it and forget it. But like the devil or cancer it eats away at you and causes us to self-mutilate through the whole course of our lives. Because the devil does not play fairly, he feels no sympathy and hates the core essence of who we are as humans. Children get nothing but suffering, pain and destruction from this weak-minded behavior.

pedophile | ˈpedəˈfīl | (Brit. paedophile)
noun
a person who is sexually attracted to children.
ORIGIN from pedo- 1 + -phile .

I will deal more with this topic in a later chapter.

When I was eleven or twelve I remember hearing the footsteps every Wednesday night. That is the night my sister would go bowling or that's what she said anyway. One night as I hear the footsteps climbing the stairs I had an idea. He always thinks I'm sleeping. *I wonder what he would do if he thought I wasn't?* So as he's about to enter my bedroom, I started coughing. The footsteps stopped... then they started disappearing back down the stairs. This happened one more time and again, I started coughing and again the footsteps disappeared back down the stairs.

That was the last time, I ever had to deal with his sickness.

5

MY STEPDAD

He loved me dearly — like a daughter.

A couple months before our mother passed away, we all moved to our oldest sister's rented farmhouse with her son, Dudie (my nephew) and her boyfriend Roger, who I consider my stepdad. We lived with an old man we called Grandpa. It was a two-story house on a very large piece of property. There were lots of trees and other buildings like barns and sheds to store the farm equipment. I remember that there was a pond way in the back of the property, and that we had a go-cart that we enjoyed riding on. I was only between two and four years old at the time, so I don't remember a lot of details except for one particular night.

If you stood at the doorway of my bedroom, there was a window directly in front of the door and a set of bunk beds to the left. The bottom bed was Dudie's and the top was mine. I remember this, because I fell out of bed one night as a child. Dudie was eight months younger than I, so he got the lower bunk.

I was upstairs playing on the floor of my bedroom with some blocks. I believe I was alone in the room at the time. All of a sudden, I heard some knocking on my window. It was a man, but I did not recognize him. He looked kind of mean, and I remember feeling afraid. He told me to open the window that was actually locked. (Thank God.). I had never opened a window lock before, so I did not know how to do it. He kept pointing to a latch, but I could not turn it or even seem to know how to turn it. He began to raise his voice. I guess he was getting frustrated with my lack of understanding or ability to do as I was told. At that moment, one of my brothers must have heard something. He came out of his room and saw the man at my window and darted off down the stairs. The man at the window stopped talking to me and disappeared.

For years, I never knew what happened to that man at the window.

Fast forward…

I am now 19 years of age and presently in Bible School, visiting my stepfather (my oldest sister's ex-husband) in Milwaukee for the weekend. I loved this man more than my own father, and in his eyes, I can do no wrong. I was his Princess, and he was the closest thing to a dad I knew.

I didn't judge him for smoking two packs of Pall Malls and drinking martinis for breakfast every morning. He swore like a sailor and thought that children were to be seen and not heard. He told me, "Do as I say and not as I do." For many years, he raced stock cars, and could be mean when he wanted to be.

In my mind, none of this mattered. I loved him anyway. He taught me, "Most men are not to be trusted." He said, "They will tell you anything you want to hear just to get in your pants, Helen. Don't fall for their smooth talking ways unless you truly know they love you and then and only then, is it okay." I believe he spoke from experience because he truly was one of those bad boys, himself. Strip joints and bars were his favorite hang-outs. I believed he could take a car apart and put it back together blindfolded. Yes, I knew he was no angel, but I also knew one thing about him: He loved me dearly—like a daughter. I was his Princess, even at 19 years of age. He taught me about cars, bars, and men. There are things I believe ALL women should be taught before moving out of Mom and Dad's house.

Things like:
• How to change your oil in your car
• How to fix a flat tire
• The names of all the tools in the toolbox
• How to prime your car if you run out of gas (old carburetors)
• How to shut down a car motor with a led pencil
• The names of the motor parts
• How to physically stop a man, if you are being attacked
• How to drive a car at age 12 (that is when I started driving him around)

One weekend when I was visiting, I walked into the kitchen and he was sitting at the table. He said, "Good morning, Princess. Did you have a good night's sleep?" I said, "Yes," as I was getting a coffee cup from the cabinet. Then I asked him, "I don't know if you remember this or not, but long ago back on the farm, a strange man was knocking at my bedroom window and yelling at me." His eyes got as big as saucers, as he put his Martini glass down on the table and said, "You remember that?" I said, "Yes, who was he?" He said, "He was an escaped prisoner from the prison a few miles from the farm. Somehow he found his way to the farmhouse, and he was obviously up to no good, because he didn't knock on the front door for help. He climbed up on the balcony above the front door to try and get into your kid's bedroom. Helen, you were only three years old, so that S.O.B. was up to no good. Could you imagine what he could of done to you if he had gotten in and took you off to the woods? If your brother hadn't walked by and saw him, there's no telling if you would be alive today." I asked him, "What did you do?" "We got our shotguns and went after him. He was an escaped prisoner—from a prison! I don't think he was in there for good behavior, do you?" He then said, "We never found him, but we chased him for hours and made sure he would not find his way back."

My stepdad is the ONLY man to this day, that I can say I truly loved as a child and knew he loved me. Bad boy or not, I knew he had my back... no matter what. In a world of endless disappointments and heartbreaks, believe me...
IT MATTERS!

Roger found out when I was older that I had been molested at a young age. He asked me, "Who touched you?" When I told him he was madder than a hornet. He confronted two of them at the same time. He told me they told him, "If you ever tell anyone, we will kill you!"

This is not a made up story people, this really is part of my past. Sounds like something out of a horror movie... right?

Secrets are what the devil loves. Keeping dirty things in the dark, allows the sin to fester like a big pile of manure. Telling people and being an open book has allowed me to see the light and to see what kind of darkness, I lived with in my past. But what can happen to a big pile of manure if it gets the sunlight it needs?

It can be the perfect place for a beautiful seed.

- Allowing God in my life is the light I needed.
- Allowing myself a prayer life and reading his word is the nourishment to feed that seed.
- Taking on the character of Christ and forgiving is the exact environment the seed needed to grow into a Beautiful Warrior for God.
- No more fear
- No More pain
- No more betrayal
- No more hiding
- No more secrets
- I am free from my broken past today, tomorrow, and forever more.

DON'T STOP NOW, THIS BOOK IS FULL OF VICTORY!

6

HOW I SPENT MY SUMMER VACATIONS

We didn't complain.

Every summer from age 7 to 12, my brothers and I would go to our Auntie and Uncle's farm. My Auntie is an awesome little Christian German lady who could cook and also baked like nobody's business. It didn't matter what she made— we always loved it, and no one could make it better. From German potato salad to my favorite dessert, poppy seed torte, she could cook! I don't ever remember her complaining about anything, and she never stopped moving around, from what I could see. She was always busy. I remember times I would be upstairs playing a game with Dudie (my nephew) for hours. We would come downstairs and find no one in the house. We would run outside and find Auntie Helen bent over in the garden picking weeds in the hot summer sun. She would have a big straw hat on her head and a smile on her face. She was just always happy to see us. So, Dudie and I would help, but we never had smiles on our faces. I never understood how she did that. It didn't really matter what she was doing—she always just seemed to be happy.

I would help my Auntie collect eggs in the morning and feed the chickens. Feeding the cows was the most fun for me because we got to fill a big cart from the ground feed chute and wheel it around the barn. I guess I liked it because it reminded me of a car. Sometimes I would hang on while Auntie would push it and give me a little ride in between stops. Sometimes they would put on the radio when we were milking the cows and polka music would fill the air. Remember, I told you they were German. I wasn't kidding! I have a few summers of polka music listening under my belt. Dudie and I used to swing each other around by our arms and sing, "Swing your partner 'round and 'round, shove him in the toilet, and flush him down."

My brothers would get up at 5:30 a.m. every morning to go help milk the cows. Dudie and I got to sleep in the first few years because there was enough help— or maybe because we were just too young. When I hit the age of ten, that luxury went away. I remember one of my favorite jobs was to feed the calves and when done, I would help carry milk from the barn to the milking parlor. I mean, the old fashioned way, in stainless steel buckets, one in each hand. Then we'd lift the buckets of milk into the bulk tank one bucket at a time until all the cows had been milked. We would do this twice a day, every day, rain or shine. We didn't complain. We knew what was expected of us, and why we were there.

7

AN EDUCATION I DIDN'T NEED

I have no understanding of this weird thing.

There were a lot of things that happened during the summers at that farm that were not fun for me. I saw a lot of things that a little girl's eyes at age 7 to 12 should never have to see. Most of these were acts done by a bunch of brothers who worked on the farm. I am not going to go into detail, but I don't feel I need to.

I will tell you that before I left that farm at age 12, I saw just about everything there was to see and know about sex except for sexual diseases. I learned about that in grade school health class. No one touched me on the farm, but there was another girl there, about four years older than I, who got their attention. They treated her in a very demeaning and sometimes torturous way. It actually taught me to withdraw within myself and become a bit of an introvert. A lot goes on in the mind when you hear and see things you shouldn't.

THE NEIGHBOR BOY

One day, my sister (who I called Mom), needed to visit with our Auntie's neighbor. To this day, I really don't know why. The neighbor had a son named Johnny who was about eight years older than I, and Dudie and I both knew him from past visits at Auntie's farm. All of us were upstairs in their house except Johnny who was not there. Dudie and I decided to go downstairs to possibly find him and see what he was doing. When we saw him, Johnny asked us if we would like to play hide-and-seek. Dudie and I both said, "Sure."

Johnny told Dudie to go upstairs and count to 100. He followed Dudie to the stairs. I heard the door shut and then the lights suddenly went off. The next thing I know, Johnny is in front of me and tells me to be quiet as he pulls my pants down and licks me down there. My mind is so confused. What is it with this licking thing boys do, and why? It doesn't last long, because I hear Dudie yelling, "One hundred," as the door opens at the top of the stairs. Johnny pulls up my pants and tells me to run into the bathroom to hide.

I have no understanding of this weird thing going on, but I think my family members will be mad at Johnny when I tell them about it. I confided in two of them, explaining what happened to me. To my dismay, they looked as confused as I was. Do they not understand why he did that, either?

A few weeks later, one of my family members caught me looking at a box of jacket patches in a shoebox on his bookshelf. He asked me if I liked any of them. I tell him, "Yes, the one that has the skunk on it." He said, "You can have it if you let me do what Johnny did to you."

I really wanted it, but not at that expense. I finally gave in, not knowing why. This happened a couple of more times, but I was sickened by the fact that I was no different than the girl who was violated on Auntie's farm. I told my family member, "This is the last time." He tried to argue with me by repeatedly asking, "Why?" I held my ground and said, "JUST BECAUSE."

It stopped, but now the guilt comes from wondering why I didn't stop it sooner. I got nothing from it. Children at that age do not get aroused. It was a stupid thing to be doing. What a waste of time.

THE LAWYER

For some reason, on this particular day, I ended up being home alone with my sister. I headed down the stairs to find out that everyone else in the family was gone. My sister, who I always called 'Mom', says to me, "My attorney is coming over to visit in a few minutes." I kindly replied with a question, "Why?" She says, "Oh, he wants to visit with us!" I say, "Okay" and run back upstairs. A half an hour or so later, I hear them talking and laughing downstairs. Then I hear my name called. "Helen, would you come downstairs, please?" I reluctantly came down the stairs and was greeted with, "Hi, how are you?" We make small talk at the dining room table when the lawyer says to me, "Do you want to play a game of hide-and-seek?" I remember that it seemed kind of weird to me. A full-grown man, standing six foot plus, wants to play hide-and-seek with me—a seven-year old! I decided to play along with him as he says, "Go hide upstairs and I will count down from 100."

I take off running, as I hear "100, 99, 98, 97, 96." My adrenaline is pumping as the race for time is against me. I can't make a decision on where I want to hide. My bedroom floor had a piece of plywood that lifted up to a hidden staircase into the drop ceiling. I contemplated going there or the closet, but I thought that if I did go into the hidden staircase, I could be trapped by him. So... I chose the closet.

I hear his footsteps climbing the staircase as I hear my heartbeat increasing louder and louder in my head. I am crouched down in a corner under a coat. I hear the wooden door slide open, and I hear him say, "I see you!" My heart sinks as he uncovers me, grabs my arm aggressively and pulls me to my feet. He whispers in my ear, "Now, you must pay for being found."

He throws me on the nearest bed, and before I know it, my pants were down.

All I am going to say is that, with his hands over my mouth, he violated me very aggressively.

But wait. There is more. He showed up again three months later, and again the same circumstance. I was home alone with my sister (go figure). This time, I knew exactly what I was in for, and being a victim of him once was quite enough for me. I vowed to myself to find a spot to hide where he would never find me.

There was a spare bedroom on the other side of the staircase, opposite to my bedroom. It's completely filled with extra furniture—all the way to the door. I dropped down on my hands and knees and crawled through the legs of the tables and chairs until I reached the back of the room. There was a big, old sewing machine there with wooden drawers. I pulled them open, and was just small enough to climb inside. I knew that this time there would be no finding me by a six-foot giant.

The "lawyer" searched and searched for well over half an hour, to no avail. Finally, I heard his footsteps go back down the stairs. I waited for a good five minutes after that before coming out. I walked halfway down the staircase, sat on the stairs, and smiled at him. I ran back up the stairs, went into my room, and locked the door.

8

FUN TIMES

Dying was not on our list of things to do.

We did work a lot on the farm, but we did have a lot of fun, too. I remember one day a storm was rolling in, and Dudie and I went outside to play in the cow pasture. He said something to me that I didn't think was too funny. So, I ripped open a cow pie and scooped up the inside and, as he was walking away, I nailed him right in the middle of his back. I busted out laughing and took off running. I was laughing so hard—I could barely run. He caught up to me and hit me right in the arm with a cow pie. We went back and forth looking for cow pies to throw at each other. We both were laughing because we looked and smelled horrible!

As we were walking back home laughing at what we had just done to each other, I stopped and said, "Dudie, listen!" We could hear pounding rain but it wasn't raining on us. Then we looked ahead and we could see a wall of rain heading straight for us. "Wow, how cool," we thought. We smiled, looked at each other, and at the same time took off running toward the wall of rain. With our hands out and our faces up in the air waiting for the rain to hit us, we started jumping up and down and dancing all around in the rain. We were wiping our clothes with our hands to get the cow pie off. We looked like drowned rats, but we didn't care. We were getting if off of us. Besides, now we didn't have to explain the nasty smell on our clothes.

I remember another time when we got this brilliant idea to push a big piece of concrete pipe up the cow pasture hill. Dudie and I rolled this thing up the hill and the idea was that both of us were to get in it and roll down the hill together. Oh, did I forget to tell you there were big rocks at the bottom of the hill as well as in the drainage ditch? It took the two of us a whole lot of effort to get it up the hill, then we put a rock or two in the front so it wouldn't roll back down as we took a rest. When we were ready, we pulled the rocks away to free it, and I told Dudie to get in, and I would hold it from rolling. Once he was ready, I jumped in and we started to roll down the hill together. Faster and faster, it started to roll. Oh... my... gosh! We got tossed around like we were in a cement mixer and it wasn't very fun anymore. I actually fell out and when I got up off the ground, I saw it rolling. I mean, fast! I noticed that it was headed for some very big rocks at the bottom. I took off, running after it, and when I caught up to it, I dragged my hands on top of it to slow it down. I actually got it to stop but only a foot or so away from a big rock at the bottom. Dudie got out pretty shook up with some bumps and bruises. We both decided that we should not do that again. It was not as fun as we had thought it would be, and dying, for that matter, was not on our list of things to do. We laughed at the end, but I think it was out of fright and relief more than anything.

Speaking of dying, there was another near-death experience when I almost killed Dudie on a tractor. Well, that is the way he sees it, anyway. I see it a little differently. I actually saved him from dying. My job was to take Dudie across the street, up to the field on top of the hill, with the big John Deer tractor. He was to pick up a tractor and wagon that was already up there. This particular tractor didn't have the big fenders above the wheels like most tractors did. It had short fenders, with hardly anything to hold on to. So, I got on and started up the tractor, and Dudie jumped on and leaned on what little fender it had on the right side. I looked both ways before crossing the street and came to a rolling stop at the end of the driveway. The road was kind of long, and then went up a pretty steep hill. As we started to climb the hill, the tractor started to slow down quite a bit, so I put the clutch in and put it into sixth gear. Then I hit the gas. Well, the front end popped up and Dudie went flying off the fender. In the corner of my eye, I saw him falling off the tractor, so with my left hand wrapped around the steering wheel, I leaned back and grabbed him by the front of his shirt and pulled him back on! You would think that he would be grateful for saving his life but he was madder than a hornet and started yelling and telling me he would never ride on a tractor with me again. You know—he never did. From that day forward, he always made me ride while he drove. I am a lot older now, and do understand what happened. Although, I still laugh out loud when I think about it today.

9

LEARNING TO RIDE SAVED MY LIFE
"Lady, you should be dead"

The old farm is where I learned to ride motorcycles at age ten. In fact, it had a race track and three or four of those little Honda mini-bikes. This is where I also learned to crash the bike properly, if there is such a thing, and it actually saved my life later in 2014 when a car pulled out in front of me as I was riding my Harley.

At an intersection in Treasure Island, Florida, the light had just turned green and I had the obvious right of way. This is when I saw a car's front bumper protruding from the SUV in the left lane. I locked up both brakes and squealed toward the silver car. I was only three car-lengths from her, and knew that I was coming in way too fast to ever avoid this accident. Hitting her straight on would mean flying over her car, doing about 25-35 mph to hit the concrete road with only the protection of a helmet.

So… at the last second, I turned my bike sideways and laid my bike alongside of her car. The remainder of the force threw me up over the handlebars, doing a summersault, and landing on my back in the middle of the intersection. I closed my eyes for a brief moment thinking, "Again, Lord?"

I heard a lady screaming and then I heard someone else say, "She's dead!" I opened my eyes to find five or six people standing over me. I started to raise my head, and I saw my bike about ten feet from where I was lying. I tried to get up, but something was wrong with my knee. I needed help.

A man ran over from across the street and said, "I saw the whole thing, and lady, you should be dead." He went on and on. "You were coming in way too fast to survive this, and if you had HIT that car, you would have never made it." My response was simple.

"I know, thank God."

I don't know how to explain in words how the brain works at laser speed. I remember approaching the car at 35 mph with both brakes locked. My thought process ran through the options in lightening speed.

1st Option: Hit car straight on
Not an Option: Moving too fast; will die

2nd Option: Maneuver around silver car
Not an Option: Can't; SUV is in the way

3rd Option: Turn bike and hit car sideways
Best Option: Possible to survive

I actually waited a brief second before turning the bike and hitting her, choosing Option 3. This thought process happened so fast—I remember having to wait until the last half-second to get about a car's length away to turn my bike. AMAZING how the brain works! When I hit that car, it was like everything went in fast-forward speed. As I went flying in the air, I tucked my head down to complete the summersault and I landed on my back. This was the only way to land and receive the least amount of damage to my body. I remember waiting for my legs and feet to follow the rest of my body and land on the road.

What an absolutely AMAZING experience to live through in life.

10

SWEET SIXTEEN

You are not alone.

Let's talk suicide. My guess is that there isn't one adult living on this earth who hasn't at least thought of it at one time or other. I really don't think it's a bad thing. It's just your mind looking at all the options in this life.

Well, my story starts again somewhere around my 16th year of life. Like I said, it really was the worst year for me. I had gotten into so many fights and arguments at home with the one who was raising me. I had just had enough. My sister's son, Dudie, was in his bedroom, which was on the other side of my door. He is eight months younger than I am, and has always been more of a brother to me than my actual blood brothers. Dudie and I have been through a lot together.

On this day, the devil was right there trying to get me to give it all up. "Boy, if you would just kill yourself, that will be the ultimate payback to her. She (my oldest sister I always called Mom), will blame herself for your death and she will feel horrible forever."

And, all of that vial, spewing anger about cost me my life.

I was upstairs in my bedroom, sitting Indian-style on the floor, with a razor blade in my right hand. I was crying. I just wanted some relief in life. I was literally at the end of my limit with everything. I just could not take even a tiny bit more. I was done playing this game of life and was ready to throw all my chips in. I had the devil on my left shoulder telling me, "Just do it!" God was on my right side saying, "Stop, and think a minute. You don't want to do this. You're better than this, Helen. I died for you. I love you!" Tears pouring down my face, I poked the blade into the vein of my left wrist. I was thinking, "All I have to do is pull it down, that's it…I'm done." I hear a voice, "Come on! Do it!" Then, "No. Stop and listen to me, Helen!"

"Think about this for one minute, I mean think it through. Say you do it? Then what? I am thinking, Dudie is in the other room. My sister is not going to find me—Dudie is! And, if he finds me, Dudie will blame himself for this, for not coming into my room sooner, or for maybe not saving me. He will find me in a massive pool of blood. He will have to live with this for the rest of his life—

blaming himself. This is not at all how I wanted this to go down..."OK... OK. I won't do it."

I slowly pulled the blade away from my wrist as a drop of blood started to slowly leak out of my skin. A part of me was relieved and exhausted, while another part of me feels so let down. I fell backwards onto my bedroom floor and started to cry uncontrollably. The pain, confusion, and massive heartache totally sucked all the energy out of me. I was lying there in relief, realizing something—I had made the right decision.

Do you see what happened? For a moment, I took my selfish eyes off of myself for the first time and realized how bad this would have turned out. Dudie was NOT the one causing my pain, and NOT the one I was trying to hurt. My sister was. This would have gone down horribly wrong.

For many of you out there who are thinking suicide as an option, please listen to me very carefully. Life is no joke, and neither are you. You are not alone, although you may feel that way at times. Open your eyes and look around you. There are plenty of others who have it much worse than you. The devil is betting his soul on your life being in vain. Don't listen to him. He is the biggest liar, thief, and con-artist alive and believe me, he is alive and well. It would please him to no end, to see you end your own life for his sake. You may not believe there is a God, and if that's where you're at, I want you to try something. I did it when I wasn't sure, myself. I called God out. Right or wrong, I desperately needed an answer. In my chapter entitled, Calling God Out, I ask Him to prove himself to me. If you do choose to do this, please remember WHO you are calling out. He will not take it lightly, and I guarantee you, HE will answer you.

I have a couple poems I want to share with you. It was where I was at the time, and they became very real to me.

TIME

Time cannot be stopped or slowed down.
It is an endless thing, I have found.
It's the constant ticker on the clock,
It's the bunny hop to sudden rock.
Time itself cannot be measured,
At any distance or space.
It's just something we learn to live with, or face.

Whether you live or die, it does not matter.
Time's hourglass will not shatter.
We're here for a reason it's true,
But time will not stop without you.

-Helen On Wheelz 6/30/83

I remember writing this poem in high school and boy, did the last four lines hit me hard. But it's so very true, time stops for NO ONE. No matter how bad you are hurting, you will never win by giving up your time here.

DOING IT FOR YOURSELF

Whenever you are down and hurt inside,
You must get up and fight, not run and hide.
For life holds only one you,
Doing it right the first time is the clue.
Many people gripe, moan, and complain,
But what are they doing about their so-called pain?
For everyone gets hurt, it's only life, they say,
But what good is life it you can't enjoy it today?
And if by chance you are pushed to the floor,
Get off your seat and don't head for the door.
For in this life you'll see,
There's only one you and only one me.
Don't think about what you don't have,
But of what you do.
That way doing it for yourself,
you will make it through.

-Helen On Wheelz

I am no rocket scientist, but I do know God has a purpose for EVERYONE of us. My question to you is: How are you supposed to know what it is, if you don't even talk to Him? I am going to be straight up and honest with you. I should not be here today! I had less than a 50/50 shot of making the right choice that night. I was in such a tremendous amount of pain, and I had already taken the razor blade into my wrist. All I really had to do was pull and no one would have been able to save me. I knew what I was doing. I had thought it out thoroughly. I am not one to make that mistake—there would have been only ONE attempt for me. What stopped me was just hearing God out, and what he said made sense. At that point, I realized that the devil almost won. He was feeding off my anger, and believe me, I had plenty of that. It was enough to kill even myself.

I want to explain something to you that my pastor's brother, James, told me when I was working with him one afternoon. He said, "Helen, do you understand that when Lucifer was sitting so close to God and found out that he was going to be under us, he was outraged. God is first, Jesus Christ, His Son and the Holy Spirit. Then, when the Christians go to heaven, they are ranked higher than the angels, so Lucifer, God's highest angel, would be beneath all of us. This infuriated him to no end and he rose up vowing to be higher and more powerful than God."

If you are a born-again Christian, you will one day be higher than the angels because we are heirs to the throne through the precious blood shed for our sins through God's son, Jesus Christ. We receive The Holy Spirit, it lives in us, so actually we ARE God's children. I mean, we are really heirs to His throne!!

How can any REAL Christian ever really have a bad day knowing THAT?

When I took my selfish eyes off of myself for just one moment, I seemed to see a light at the end of a tunnel. When I lifted up my head and truly opened my eyes to look around, I realized there wasn't even a tunnel there in the first place. I had been crawling on the floor with my eyes shut, banging my head on the wall.

STAND UP!!
LOOK UP!!

Know that God will take your hand at any time. All I did was reach for His. I picked up His Word (The Bible) and started reading. Yes, it does take effort. But HE was ALWAYS there... waiting for me to make the tiniest move! I drew closer and closer to Him and today... Today I have nothing but peace and tranquility. My love for God is so satisfying and fulfilling. I don't even need or want a mate. Don't get me wrong, I am still human but I have asked Him to take my worldly desires from me (they were bothersome), and He has done so. Some day, maybe after this book is finished, I will desire to have a mate. But right now, I am at total peace with focusing on just me.

This is my sacrifice to help YOU!

I may not know you personally, but through Christ
I still love every one of you (God's people).
God loves You... He made YOU.
Jesus loves You... He died for your sins.
The Holy Spirit Loves You... He lives IN YOU once You accept Christ into your life.

I Love YOU. I'm giving up part of my life to write this book for YOU.

Don't you think... IT'S TIME TO START LOVING YOURSELF?

11

WALLS

Walls, they're there to protect you.

I had made a decision in my life at one point to let no one hurt me ever again. *(When I say that, I mean to the point of breaking my spirit or devastating me.)*

I really don't know how old I was or even what got me to decide to do all this, but the decision was made and the walls started to go up. You might be asking, "What is a WALL?" My only explanation is that a wall is an easy pain blocker. You see, I truly believe that we, as humans, care about things enough to allow them to cause us pain. I also learned that if you stop caring, there is no pain. Someone can only hurt you if you let them. The key word here is LET or allow them to affect you.

A lot of people don't realize that we all have the power to allow pain or happiness into our lives. I think so many people think that we just have to "take it" or "accept it" just as it is. NOT SO. I have found that we have the power to control our painful moments, if we choose.

The question is: What do you choose to let into your life?
Only you can answer that by the decisions you make every day.

Because I had dealt with so much negativity in my childhood, I guess I just had enough and shut all of it off one day. Now, I only allow positive and honest people into my world, or into my heart. To be honest with you, My GOD is the only one who can hurt me to no return. I have given Him that power in my life.

That is a conscious decision on my part.

Then, there is my Son and my Grandchildren because they are a part of me, and I would truly die for them without any question if need be. Then comes the love of my life (if I have one), and my close circle of friends and some family members. Outside of that, there is really no one who can touch me, unless I (want to) let them. People will always be people, and for some reason, our selfish ways tend to hurt the ones we love the most. Sometimes, that is, even ourselves.

I'm a straight shooter, so I know where I stand with myself; I have disciplined myself that way. There is a fine line I walk in most topics of life, and I pride myself in not seeing much gray areas out there. Although I know there are a few exceptions to the rule, because I realize that God did not make robots.

I'd like to share a story with you about something that happened to me in grade school. To tell you the truth, I guess I did it subconsciously to protect myself from this happening again.

I was in the 4th or 5th grade. My birthday was approaching, and I could have a roller skating party if I wanted to, but I was only allowed to invite five girls. So, I gave invitations out to my five favorite girlfriends in school. The weekend of my party, only one girlfriend showed up. I was devastated and I let it ruin my whole day and many days thereafter. From that day on, I refused to tell anyone when it was my birthday. I really don't think they had done it intentionally—at least I don't think that now.

After that day, I started telling people I don't have a birthday. I would tell them that I was found under a rock, and they would laugh and the subject would change. I cannot tell you how many different people in my lifetime I told this to. To this day, there are people I know that do not know my birth date because for years, I refused to tell anyone.

Now, I'm 43-years old, and I just figured this out six months ago in one of my counseling sessions. I said, "I don't like people to know my birthday," My counselor asked me, "Why is that?" I said, "I really don't know!" This got me thinking on the drive home. Why don't I like people to know my birthday?

I had to dig way back to when this started—when I was young. I thought, how long have I been doing this, anyway?

Then it hit me.

I had put a protective wall up years ago by not letting anyone know when my birthday was. By doing that, I could never be hurt on that day ever again. What they don't know won't hurt me…I guess was my thought. Well, it worked, but I don't need it anymore. I am well over it now. I really don't care if people know my birthday or not.

I used this lack of knowledge as a wall for myself, and it worked to the point that I don't need it anymore. I guess maybe I have outgrown my childish concerns about this topic and have decided not to allow others to control my happiness.

I have used walls to protect myself, but I do not believe that all walls are good forever. Sometimes we use them to hinder our own growth and that is not a good wall. So, you have to know when to break them down, and when they are no longer benefiting you in a positive way.

Just like the one I just shared with you, I see no benefit in it for me anymore, so the wall has come down. I guess because I just decided that if no one remembers my birthday... it's okay. I am big enough, old enough, and mature enough that I am okay with that.

Now, I do celebrate the day God chose to give me my first breath. I celebrate, not because I worship myself, but because I honor God's gift to this world... me.

During the summer of my freshman year of high school, I was asked by my second oldest sister and her husband if I would like to spend the summer in Michigan and help her babysit my niece and two nephews? "Wow, how awesome. Yes of course I would."

It got me away from the darkness at home and was like a vacation for me. My sister and I became very close and still are today.

The following summers, I stayed outside of Milwaukee with a couple I named Roy & Sue. I babysat their six-month-old son Christopher, for two summers. I really loved it there and again it was a great getaway from the messed up home life.

I did miss Dudie but he was busy on the farm every summer.

12

JANUARY 12, 1983

I knew my sins were forgiven.

I had just gotten off the bus from high school and nobody was home yet. I walked across the street to get the mail. Speaking of my birthday, my Auntie had sent me a card. Inside the card was a tract or pamphlet, which talked about Jesus. You know, on your birthday, everything just seems a little more special throughout the day? Well, after I read the card I read the tract. I mean, I stopped whatever I was doing; I sat down and I read it word-for-word, sentence-by-sentence, and paragraph-by-paragraph. Before I was finished, tears started running down my face and I could not stop crying. I was so overwhelmed with joy that I could hardly breathe. It was a feeling I had never felt before. So secure, so comforting, so overwhelming—and warm, like a hot blanket out of the dryer had just been laid over my body on a cold winter night. I was feeling it all over me, but it wasn't just outside my body—it was inside, too.

I actually felt the Holy Spirit enter my body right then and there alone—right there in the kitchen. The Joy, the overwhelming Joy and feeling of peace and tranquility just entered my body. It was like a bolt of lightening. I was crying like a baby for five or ten minutes, trying to take it all in. "I just accepted the Lord," I thought. "I can't thank you enough, God, for accepting ME. You are so unbelievably AWESOME, GOD!" By accepting the Lord, I mean in my heart not just my head, I, for the first time, truly believed that Jesus Christ the Son of God actually and wholly died for me. I believe He would have taken the beatings, the humiliation, the nailing on the cross, the going to hell—all of it—if I had been the ONLY one on this earth.

In my heart of hearts, I knew my sins were forgiven through His blood being shed on that cross. That cross belongs to me. Not someone who knew no sin. If that doesn't humble you… nothing will. My soul was calling for me to stop, just once in my busy life, and see what He actually went through. I asked myself, "For what?

For us?

Self-centered, selfish, self-righteous, egotistical, greedy, humans?"

We don't even deserve to smell His feet much less talk to Him. But... He loves us. Ohhhhhh, How He loves us!

Can you see the FREE gift He is offering?

Do you feel the NEED for REAL peace in your life?

Do you ever wonder what REAL joy actually feels like? You can only receive that from Him... no other. He didn't have to do ANY of what He did. He did it out of LOVE and GRACE. The best thing about it is that it was done with unconditional love with no stipulations.

All of these emotions were running through my head like a boulder down a hill. I was so overwhelmed with understanding and Joy. Coming from every part of my being, filling me, 'til I couldn't take it any more. My eyes shed tears of joy, not happiness—so much deeper and meaningful than happiness. This was coming from my core being, from deep inside me. This was joy I had never felt before. What an awesome gift it is, and it comes from the Holy Spirit.

At that moment, something was telling me to go outside. I walked to the front door, opened it, and could not believe my eyes. I kept walking to the screen door and stepped out. Tears again began running down my face as I stared humbly at the sky. I cannot possibly tell you in words what I really saw there that night. I was looking at the most beautiful sunset I had ever seen in my life. It was January, and all the leaves were off the trees. We have this huge tree in the front yard that leaves a full circle of branches every winter. When that sun settled over that tree that night, I knew it was made just for me. What an Awesome, Awesome God we have! He knows our every hearts' desires—even the ones we don't talk about. Again, I began to cry, hard like a baby. These were tears of pure joy coming from my soul. I just couldn't be happier than I was at that moment. Overwhelming comes to mind, but even bigger than that word. I don't know if the English language had one. If I close my eyes and think of that moment, I can still see that sunset today.

I accepted the Lord that evening on my 17th birthday.

13

COPING WITH THE PAIN

I needed someone who accepted me for me.

I am only in fifth grade and totally the class clown. I have the power to make the whole class laugh and the teacher to look like an idiot.

I remember in one of my classes, the teacher had arranged our desks in a big circle. The teacher would talk to us while he stood in the center of the circle. As he was talking to the other side of the circle, his back was in front of me. I would stand on my chair and stick out my tongue. Then, I would put my thumbs on my ears and wave my fingers. The whole class would be rolling in laughter. And before the teacher could turn around, I would drop back into my seat with my hands on my chin. I would give him a look like, what the heck is everyone laughing at?

I remember doing this, countless times. I just enjoyed a good laugh, and I still do today. Although, back then it was at my teacher's expense, I guess I just needed a release and school was a part of it. Laughing became a way of coping with some of the pain. I think it served me very well. Don't we all enjoy a good laugh? Laughing is just pure fun, and it helped me forget about all the pain for just a moment. A way of taking a breather from all the negative that seemed to surround me.

Today, I am a very positive person. When I see a glass of water, it is always half full.

Another way I would cope with negativity in my life was by writing. I loved to write poetry. Quiet time—with me, myself, and I. Let's get down to how I really feel.

So, in a sense, I would talk it out on paper. The good, the bad, and the ugly. I am the type of person who, when I see a problem, I want to fix it. If I had a problem with another person, I would try to fix it somehow in my head by writing it down and thinking it through. So, the next time I saw that person, I would have thought it through to the point that I would know how I felt about the problem. I don't like loose ends in my friendships. Acquaintances—okay, but not with friends. No.

I am very blessed to have a lot of friends today. I mean, I have more than I should. When I was in grade school, all my friends were boys until I got to sixth grade. That is when I met my best friend, Karen, a tomboy—just like me! She had a bit of a rough home life, too and we just hit it off as friends from the very beginning. Although we were very different, she was very popular in school and I… I was just not too concerned with other people.

I just didn't care for people that much. I was more of a loner and that is how I liked it. Karen didn't care about that, and neither did I. We have always trusted each other and she can always make me laugh out loud! She likes to embarrass me if she can, and she still tries doing that today.

Back in high school, having Karen as a friend was very important to me. I needed someone who accepted me for me. We were without all the drama, rules, or stipulations that people like to put on each other. Karen and I never did these things with each other. I have always felt very accepted by her. She invited me to sleep over on weekends, just so I could get out of my house. She gave me a sense of self-worth and importance that I so vitally needed at that age. Karen actually helped me accept myself, too, if that makes sense.

A very popular person in school is what she was—good at about any sport. She was on the Homecoming Court, and dated the most popular guys in the school. Me—I was a bit of an introvert and only went out for Track and Field, sports wise. I was in a couple of acting plays, which I enjoyed, and I was Vice President of the Student Council for four years. Although I dated no one in high school, I did have a few crushes. I was not on the top, but I was not on the bottom. I was somewhere in the middle. I was nowhere near the status level of Karen.

But, it was so cool, because neither one of us cared where the other ranked as far as popularity. I think we just both treasured the honesty and loyalty we found in each other and it was enough and still is today.

I had my teacher-friend, Sherry, and one other schoolmate a few grades under me. I called her "Mouse," and I loved her like a sister. I still do, even though we don't talk. She lived about a mile from my house, and I remember sleep overs at her house as well. The whole town loved Mouse's mom, Shirley, and everyone called her "Mom."

Shirley was loved by many, and I remember talking to her at her kitchen table about some of the messed-up world I lived in. I never went too deep with details because I guess I just didn't want to make other people feel sad for me.

Other than that, I really did not get too close to anyone else. It was truly because I did not trust, and without trust… you have nothing.

I don't like drama. I'd had enough of it in my own life for everyone. So, I only hung around those who did not cause drama and liked to laugh. It's where I found my peace.

14

DRUGS AND SUICIDE

I got out of this with a little help from a friend.

I want to start off by saying that I put these two topics—drugs and suicide—in one chapter for a reason. They go together because they are both a means of destruction; one to the body and the other to the soul. Either way, we cheat ourselves out of life.

Before I get too far into this, I want to explain something. I know full well that there are many different reasons why people my think of suicide as an option. Due to the vast amount of reasons, I want to start by eliminating a few right off the bat. These are the reasons that I am NOT referring to: The first are chemical imbalances in the body. I have read that a lack of or low levels of niacin can cause chemical imbalance. A handful of cashews is a natural way to help people with this problem.

The second to eliminate from the list is the impact of medications that people are taking. I know that there are a lot of medications that are mind altering. I am NOT talking about either of these two reasons.

What I am talking about are past or present situations that make us feel a sense of hopelessness. I am talking to those who presently have or have had very dramatic childhood pasts and feel like life is just to much for them to bear.

I am going to take you into my world as a 16-year old to show you how I dealt with situations that felt hopeless at the time. I'd also like to show you how I got out of this with a little help from a friend.

I am going to share with you some poems I wrote when I was down and out, and I felt like I could go no further. I am going to show you that by shifting my eyes, I could see clearly into the future. I need to tell you that I am no expert on suicide or drugs, for that matter. All I really can tell you are my own experiences. I have been in the ring with the devil on my back, tempting me from all sides. He told me, "You need to stop the pain because no one cared about me anyway." He talked about how life is a joke and I was just the fool playing along. I was in a place where I felt that the joke was actually on me and that everyone was laughing. The pain was so unbearable that death became a comforting thought. I was in a place where I felt that I was in a tunnel and couldn't see any way out—there was only darkness. UNTIL... I OPENED MY EYES AND I COULD SEE I WASN'T EVEN IN A TUNNEL. I'D BEEN CRAWLING ALONG WITH MY EYES SHUT!!

My story starts at Sweet Sixteen which is another chapter where I have told the whole story. It was truly the worst year of my entire life. My body was going through so many changes, I didn't even know if I wanted to laugh or cry. This "being a woman thing" seriously sucked, and I hated everyone including myself. I had been repeatedly molested at my own home from the age of five to somewhere around twelve. I had a lot of friends in school, but none of them knew of my disastrous home life. It was my intention to keep it that way.

To do this, I hid my thoughts and feelings, memories, pain, and whatever else went along with my messed-up life. I tucked it far away in a place I rarely visited. I had started experimenting with some things that I thought might help. Drugs. Because caring about myself meant pain, I just stopped caring. I started off with a little vodka and soda before I caught the bus in the early morning. By the time I got to school an hour later, I was flying like a kite and laughing at just about anyone and anything. Then, a couple weeks after that, I found myself buying marijuana from a friend. I really started to enjoy this "Who gives a sh*t" attitude!" To be honest with you, I really could not feel the pain like I did when I was straight, and I started enjoying that feeling more and more. Besides, who cares anyway? I was getting awfully sick of caring. That is when I started taking speeders. They became part of my daily routine, and I thought, "No more pain!" Then my life began flying by, and I didn't know if I was coming or going anymore, but I sure was enjoying the ride... I thought.

The only problem that I saw was that I was becoming immune to the drugs I was taking, and I continued to need more as time went on. Other than that, life was good!

Then one day, my world came to a crashing halt. One of my teachers, Mrs. Baker, called me into her classroom one morning. I was actually becoming very close to this teacher. She was not like the others. She was different in a comforting and caring kind of way. There was just something about her that drew me to her and I wanted the peace I knew that she had. She meant the world to me and she had become my friend.

Mrs. Baker shut the door behind us and told me to sit down. I thought my heart was going to beat right out of my chest as I struggled to sit down in the chair. "What's up?" I said with a massive lump in my throat. She said, "Helen... I know something is going on with you." "What do you mean by that?" I asked. (I knew very well what she meant, but I didn't want to say another word.) "You've been drinking, I can smell it on your breath, and I know you well enough to know that it's more than alcohol. I don't know exactly what you're doing, because I don't know anything about that kind of stuff. I do know that you're going through a very difficult time at home because you have told me this in the past. I know you are probably hurting inside, but this is no way to fix all that—even if it may feel right. I just want you to know something. You're not just hurting yourself in all this—you're hurting me, too. I really care about you and it hurts me to see you doing this to yourself"

I swear that my heart was beating louder than her voice as I said, "It takes away the pain and it makes me feel happy."

You could hear a pin drop as silence filled the room. She waited, and then finally said, "For how long, Helen? You don't need it." Silence echoed in the room. A tear ran down my cheek. I looked her straight in the eyes and said, "You're right. I don't need this stuff. I will take care of it today." We both stood up, and I hugged her harder than I had ever hugged anyone before. I said, "Thank you." I rubbed my face dry, and walked out of the room with a whole new outlook on my life.

I went home from school that afternoon, collected all my stash and flushed it down the toilet.

I want to share something VERY PERSONAL with you. It's a song that she wrote me back then. I cannot tell you the countless times I had listened to this over and over again. It gave me a sense of being, a reason to fight through the pain, knowing that someone actually cared about me enough to take the time to write this for me.

THERE AREN'T ENOUGH WORDS

There aren't enough words for true expression,
No sufficient verses in my possession.
I could write all day and for half the night,
I could sing my songs if my mood is right.
Some would paint yet others draw,
Some create and just express it all.
Yet none would do to make you aware
Of your meaning to me.
Is it possible then to tell you,
What you mean to me?... I don't know

There aren't enough words for true expression,
No sufficient verses in my possession.
I could write all day and half the night,
I could sing my songs if my mood is right.
Some would paint yet others draw.
Some create and express it all.

Yet none would do to make you aware.
Of your meaning to me.

Is it possible then to tell you,
What you mean to me?
Or come near to what it seems?

-Sherry Baker

As I look back on what happened, I often wonder: WHY and WHAT was it that actually got me to stop?

I underlined one sentence in this chapter and it is the key to why, I felt I needed drugs or what I call a "CRUTCH". Let's look up that word and see what Dictionary says about it.

crutch | krə ch |
noun
1 a long stick with a crosspiece at the top, used as a support under the armpit by a lame person.
• [in sing.] figurative a thing used for support or reassurance : they use the Internet as a crutch for their loneliness.
2 archaic another term for crotch (of the body or a garment).

verb [intrans.]
move by means of or as if by means of crutches : I was crutching down a long corridor.

1. **Something that a person uses too much, for help or support.**
2. **Something that a person depends on, to help deal with problems.**

Wow! BINGO!

Isn't that what drugs REALLY are?

"Something that a person depends on, to help them deal with problems?"

And it all stems to the underlined words in this chapter.

I wrote this fun little poem about the time I was going through all these issues:

WASTED AWAY

Roll a joint, smoke it away.
Too far gone to remember the day.
Suck a few beers at the party tonight,
Till I'm wasted and flying like a kite.
My head hurts and I ache,
Is it worth the pills I take?
Of course not, whom I trying to fool,
It's just the image of being cool.

Wake up my friend before it's too late,
Days have gone by and ahh... .
Do you remember the date?
Why am I playing this game of mine,
Don't remember the party, and lost track of time.
Whom I livin for? It's certainly not me,
Cuz I'd stop this jiving and face reality.
I'm proud to say, no more wasted away,
For I have come back and this time to stay.

-Helen On Wheelz 9/5/1982

I also found this picture I drew and little paragraph I wrote back then, I think it fits here.

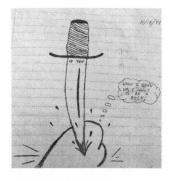

Helen,
Feelings, I hate them.
All I feel is empty pain.
Why must I feel so much pain?
What did I do to deserve this?
I was not asked to be born.
Why was I robbed like this?
It hurts, my heart hurts so bad.
I don't want this hurt anymore,
It's so heavy.
Why me?
Why!!?

I vaguely remember writing this it almost felt like I was talking about someone else and not really myself.

I want to explain something that I think is very important in all this. I realize this was my situation or experience with drugs and some of you may think, "Well I didn't go through what you did or you didn't go through what I did"... But it all stems back to PAIN. This is why we choose to self-mutilate and take up crutches.

Listen, we all have to walk in our own shoes every day. I can't be responsible for anyone else but me. Every decision we make every day affects our tomorrow. That goes for everyone.

We can make excuses for wrongful actions we make and justify them all day long, and many people do. Believe me, it all comes out in the laundry in the end. I guess what is interesting to me is the fact that when I look back on this experience in my life, I see all that it took for me to let go of the destruction, was to know that someone really cared about me—in a real sense that I REALLY mattered to someone and that **the pain was not in vain.**

It gave me the strength to carry on and face the music, no matter how bad it sounded.

It gave me a reason to face reality and not use drugs as a crutch for my pain.
It gave me the freedom to make the right decisions sober, even though some were the dumbest mistakes in the beginning.

I chose freedom over bondage; a road less traveled but one that is definitely more rewarding in the end.

I took the pain and felt it.

I learned to walk though it—like A WARRIOR.

Not disguising it.

Not hide from it, never dealing with it, until I die.

You can do this, too. It only takes your decision to do so, and the commitment to put one foot in front of the other.

Before you know it you will be running a strong race.

Another poem I wrote, looking back on God and my life:

DESTINED TO WIN

Here you are running a race,
Which seems impossible to win.
Your Coach told you "you're destined to win,
Don't give up those guys will give in".
But as you are running, you just want to die,
Your lungs hurt so bad, you begin to cry.
Your heart beat increases and your tempted to cheat,
If I step in his lane, I could win the meet.
It means a shorter distance, who would care?
But "no", that's not right and it's not fair".
You want to give up you want to stop trying,
But you know you are close to the finish line.
As you look on, it's nowhere in site,
Your coach yells, "now, push with all your might".
Your steps increase you know it's true,
He's closer now only a foot from you.
He turns to look and shocked to see,
You're neck to neck running franticly.
You see the line and your Coach is there,

"My child come to me, if you care"?
The guy on the right, slowly disappears,
The tape hits your chest and you burst into tears.
"My child you did it, you were destined to win,
You obeyed what I said and you ran from your sin"

-Helen On Wheelz 2/9/86

I Corinthians 9:24 –27 (NIV)
Do you not know that in a race all the runners run, but only one gets the prize?
Run in such a way as to get the prize. Everyone who competes in the games goes
into strict training. They do it to get a crown that will not last; but we do it to
get a crown that will last forever. Therefore, I do not like a man running aim-
lessly; I do not fight like a man beating the air. No, I beat my body and make it
my slave so that after I have preached to others, I myself will not be disqualified
for the prize.

God… IS REAL and He really loves us more that we can ever imagine. I know those words sound so cliché and you probably have heard it before. But from my experience, I can tell you: He is NO JOKE. He really does truly love us.
Think about it, why wouldn't He?
He made us; we are His creations.
You may not have anyone to turn to.
I want you to know He was there for me.
He is ALWAYS, ALWAYS there for me and
He cares for you more than you care for yourself.

I am not here to try to convince you of anything; this is just My Story, and this is how I got through the pain. I did not write this book for me; I wrote this book because my counselor told me I needed to. Here are her exact words: "Helen, you should not be sitting on my couch (statistically). You should be a drug ad-dict, prostitute, or a dead person, but you should not be living a normal life (with a job, relationship, house). I have people come in here with half the prob-lems you have gone through in life, and they can't function normally. You need to sit down and write a book. Do you know how many people you could help?"

Those are the exact words that my counselor, Mona told me.

All these countless hours of my life (typing), are to help YOU the reader. People, who have gone through some of the same things in life that I have, and some of you don't know how to get through the pain, without self – destructing or crutching.

You can do it! I am doing it!
How do you eat an elephant?
That's right.
One bite at a time... this is no different.

THE PAIN is real and I dealt with it by taking the pain (one step at a time) like a Warrior without the crutches and turned to a source stronger than myself... GOD.

Why God? Because EVERYONE else had failed me!

I just could NOT take another disappointment....not even one.
I had hit my limit and I knew it!
As God as my anchor,
I then found myself a good counselor.
There is no magic here, no hocus pocus,
Just pure grin and bear it.
Determination to power through it.
A lot of tears.
A lot of facing the truth.
A lot of praying.
A lot of joy and self –peace later,...... but it comes!!
I promise it will come through Christ.
Don't give up, keep reading and growing to become a better, stronger you.
I turned to God and found my purpose...you can too.

> *"I am NOT better than you... Just obedient."*
> *- Pastor Joey Sarlo*

James 4:4-7 (NIV)
Submit yourselves, then, to God resist the devil, and he will flee from you.
Come near to God and He will come near to you. Wash your hands, you sinners,
And purify your hearts, you double minded. Grieve, mourn and wail. Change
your laughter to mourning and your joy to gloom. Humble yourselves before
The Lord
And He will lift you up.

> *"My mind needs to be the LEARNER, not the LEADER."*
> *- Pastor Joey Sarlo*

15

CALLING GOD OUT

I am in big trouble, now I am lost.

I was 16 years of age and I remember having conflicting thoughts about who God was and if He even existed. I believe this was just a few months after my suicide battle. I know I've expressed that God was on one side and the devil was on the other; but because I didn't believe at that time, I really didn't know what or who was talking to me. Suicide was the only thing on my mind. It was just a good side and a bad side talking in my head. It's now that I am much older and looking back, that I realized what was going on at the time.

My school teacher Sherry and I, were becoming very good friends. It seemed as though we ended up talking about God a lot of the time. I remember sometimes even getting frustrated about the whole topic. I remember saying, "You have your religion and I have mine. You worship your God, and I will worship mine."

Sherry was my French/Spanish teacher in high school. She was a Christian and I was a Catholic—but hardly practicing much of anything. Her response would be, "No, I do not have a religion. I have a relationship and there is a big difference, Helen." I really did not understand what she meant by that. I felt I was a good kid, respected others, and tried to stay out of trouble for the most part. I did unto others as I would have wanted done unto me. I tried my best not to lie, steal or harm anyone. I believed in God the best I could, for not seeing Him face to face. I talked to Him when I thought I needed to or was in trouble for some reason. God was cool I thought, and definitely someone to look up to. I remember as a young kid singing the song, *This Little Light of Mine* at the neighbor's house, but other than that, I really didn't know much at all.

Sherry was the type of person who just had that something special about her that appealed to me—a calm soothing spirit. I wanted to have the same inner peace. I could see it and feel it when around her, but I didn't know how to get it. She intrigued me and seemed so knowledgeable about the Bible and life. I was amazed at her ability to quote a verse from the Bible on just about any topic. I remember thinking, *What is it about her that makes me feel so comfortable?* I could talk to her about anything. She was not like the other teachers in school. She was different in a calm, truly caring kind of way.

I wanted to find out what she had. The more I got to know her, the more I was being driven to find it. I trusted her like I had trusted no one before. I knew I could trust her with anything. She was more mature than my other friends, and I didn't have to play stupid head games. She would listen to me without judging, and I knew whatever was said was safe with her. I think my level of maturity was higher than my friends anyway, because of what I had already gone through in my life. She was an adult and had already graduated from college. She was married and was only seven years older than I. It seemed as though she was an angel God had sent to me after all I had been through as a child. I never told her that, but I truly believe it to this day. I owe her dearly for taking time to help me through the darkest hours of my life. I realize it was God, working through her to get to me, but she will always be someone that I would die for, if need be.

One night in November, (I remember the month because deer hunting season starts in November), I was in bed praying to God. I said, "Lord are you really up there? Do you really hear me? If you are really real, I need you to prove yourself to me. You want me to give my life to you. You want me to give you my time, and all that I am, but I don't really know if you are even real. I cannot see you or talk to you like a real person. Yet, my friend Sherry tells me that you are real. I am asking you to show yourself to me somehow."

Please listen when I tell you to be very careful what you ask for. This was NOT taken lightly by Him and as you will see it changed my life forever.

Two weeks later, I found myself in the woods—deer hunting. I started hunting when I was 13 years old. (OK, I am a little redneck.) Anyway, I had been in the woods from 5:00 a.m. until about 1:00 p.m. I came in to get warmed up and also stock up on a few chocolate bars for energy. When I got to the house, my nephew Dudie was there. I told him I had seen a deer that morning but could not get a good shot. He asked, "Can I come out with you?" I said, "OK." So we got ready, and within five minutes, we were out the door.

I took Dudie to the exact place I had seen the deer that same morning and showed him the deer blind (a shelter built of sticks and leaves) I had built. We had made an agreement (because I was the only one with a watch), that at 4:00 p.m. I would fire my gun off at a tree and we would walk back to the house together.

I watched Dudie disappear into the woods and about 30 minutes later, I heard him say, "I'm going in now." I'm thinking, because we had only been out there like 30 minutes, he meant to say 'I'm going into the woods now." I respond with an "OK," as I am sitting very still waiting for my big deer to show himself.

Two hours or so went by, and 4:00 p.m. comes around on my watch. So I start yelling, "Dudie!" I'm thinking maybe I won't have to fire my gun; maybe he's close enough to hear me yell. I wait for a response, and I hear nothing. So I fire my gun off at a tree—like I told him I would do. **BANG!!**

I wait again to hear some kind of noise—maybe branches breaking and Dudie walking toward me, but I hear nothing. So I yell again, "DUDIE, DUUUDIE!" I wait. I hear nothing, and he's not yelling back or anything. I am really starting to worry now. He should have heard my gunshot for miles. I am thinking, "Could he be lost in the woods?" So I yell louder and started walking to where I had seen him disappear into the woods two plus hours before. I continued to yell, "DUDIE WHERE ARE YOU?" I waited... no answer. I kept walking—hoping to hear something. It was getting darker as daylight was coming to a fast close. I turned around, and thought I needed to go home to let them know that Dudie is lost in the woods. When I realized that nothing looked familiar to me from where I was standing, I looked down, thinking I can follow my footprints back to my deer blind. As I looked down I realized there are footprints everywhere. I think, *Oh no, I am in big trouble, now I am lost.* I tried to walk back to find my deer blind, but seemed to be totally disoriented to the point I didn't know which way was north or south anymore. I could barely see the sunlight and couldn't tell where it was setting. My only thought was, *I only have five shotgun shells left. There are bears out here and it's getting very cold.*

I began to panic and realized my desperation and need to get out of the woods fast before all light is gone. I yell, "HELP!! HELP!" and waited to listen. Wait a minute I hear something... I can't make out the words but someone is yelling back to me. I start to walk towards the sound. So I yell again, "HELP!! HELP!!" I stop and listen. Yes, I hear a voice!

I started walking toward the sound. Then I stopped!! I began to think, *We own 40 acres of this woods. That voice has got to be coming from the other side somewhere. I am going deeper into the woods instead of getting out. I cannot follow that voice I may never get out of here, by the time the sun goes down. I turn away from it and really start to realize how alone I am.* I panicked, and started to run in desperation to get out quickly. I ran into a swampy area, and as I was running, my foot went in between two branches, and I fell into the water. The gun was in my right hand, and as I lay in the water, the gun was pointed at my head. *My God,* I am thinking *I could have blown my head clean off.*

I begin to cry, and yell out loud, "GOD HELP ME, I CAN'T SPEND THE NIGHT IN THE WOODS ALONE, HELP ME PLEASE!!" I was sick to my stomach from fright. I have never been so desperate in my whole life.

If you have never been afraid for your life before, let me be the first to tell you how unbelievably humbling it is. It will break you down to the point of total humility like nothing you ever experienced before. There was no pride left in me and I had no choice left but to trust in God. No one was left to trust in or even hear me for that matter. Who would have thought this a few months ago when I was ready to die and end it all? Now look at me—fighting with everything in me to survive.

I get up soaking wet, crying, and totally humbled. I walked out of the swamp and spied a hill. I start to climb the hill, and when I got to the top I saw a clearing with no trees. It looked like a perfect round circle—no trees were there! I walked to the middle of the clearing and dropped to my knees.

The butt of the gun was in the ground as I was leaning on the barrel with both hands, I closed my eyes.

"MY GOD!! IF YOU ARE UP THERE, I AM BEGGING YOU TO PLEASE HELP ME GET OUT OF HERE. I AM SO LOST AND SCARED. I DON'T WANT TO SPEND THE NIGHT IN THE WOODS ALONE. I AM SOAKING WET AND FREEZING COLD. PLEASE, PLEASE HELP ME GET OUT OF HERE, PLEASE."

I opened my eyes and lifted my head up. My mouth dropped open—I could not believe what my eyes were looking at. I knew this was not here when I put my head down. It couldn't have been—I would've seen it. As I look through the trees and I could see the sun setting in the distance, I said out loud, "MY GOD, YOU REALLY ARE REAL, THANK YOU LORD JESUS."

All the symbols were there for me that night. I saw the sun through the trees, symbolizing the Son of God. He also knew that I knew how to get home from that one symbol. You see, the sun always sets on the other side of the road in front of our house. Do you get it...? Follow the sun (SON) to get home.

It changed my life in that I have no doubt of God's existence and I never will again. That night was a night I will remember for the rest of my life.

16

TRIP TO MARYLAND

That's how we learn.

It was the summer of 1984, and I had just graduated from high school. I had wanted to become an actress since I was 12 years old. (To be honest, I had wanted one of two different things, to become an actress or truck driver.) I had just contacted a couple of schools; one in New Jersey and one in Maryland, but New Jersey was such a big city to me that it literally scared me to even think about it. Maryland... now doesn't that sound like a nice quaint place? It sounded like *Merry Land* to me; you know, *Happy Land*. So, my decision was made—Maryland it is.

I was going to Towson State University to study Pantomime, Choreography, Drama, and Acting. This course was a four-credit course. It was a summer course, and I had plans to live on campus. After the school accepted me, I drove down to the bus station and bought my ticket to that happy place. I prepared myself to leave in the next few weeks. For someone who was going on this big adventure by myself, I did not seem to have a single fear.

The morning I was to leave, I put on a pair of men's white shorts with red trim (little did I know this was not a smart choice of clothing), a red T-shirt and a nice, new pair of tennis shoes. I weighed about 130 pounds soaking wet with a head full of black curly hair.

My friend Sherry took me to the bus station that morning to catch the bus out. I remember getting on the bus and seeing a man sitting in the front seat behind the bus driver. He gave me that look. You know ladies—that up and down look some men give when they are too stupid to think straight. He was an older Hispanic man who looked out of place to me. He was wearing older wrinkled clothes that looked like they needed a washing. I really didn't think much of him, as I went about my business toward the back of the bus. I found a row of empty seats on the left side of the bus, and I couldn't wait to sit down. Aahh, my adventure was about to begin, I thought. I still remember looking out the window and seeing my friend Sherry standing there looking up at me. I still remember the last thing she said to me as the bus was pulling out. In fact I can still see her vividly in my mind to this day. She pointed to her eye, tapped her heart with her fingers and pointed at me. That was our way of saying I love you without words. I did the same back to her, and at that very moment I realized I was ALONE. I felt a little cautious or uneasy as she faded away in the distance, yet it felt like this was something I had to do.

We stopped at a truck stop. The bus driver said over the intercom, "In a half hour, I will be pulling this bus out of here, and not a minute later. You have exactly half an hour." We all got up and left as fast as possible without touching each other. I went straight to the bathroom. I prefer regular bathrooms to what that bus had to offer. Then I went to get myself a Coke, a candy bar and a bag of shelled sunflower seeds. I sat down at a booth for about ten minutes, enjoying my Coke and sunflower seeds and the view of the truck stop. I put the candy bar in my pocket for later and walked out to get my seat on the bus. The Hispanic man was sitting at a booth, and I had noticed him looking at me a few different times. He tried to talk to me in Spanish as I walked by, but I smiled and said, "I don't speak Spanish" and kept walking. I got back to my seat on the bus and waited about five minutes when the bus driver said, "Did anyone see that Hispanic fella that was sitting behind me?" A couple people raised their hands and the bus driver looked back at me. "Would you do me a favor and go tell him the bus is leaving?" I looked around to see if he could be talking to someone else. I pointed to myself. The bus driver said, "Yes, could you please?" I smiled and said, "Yes," as I realized I was the only one on the bus, besides the Hispanic man, who even looked Hispanic.

So I jumped off the bus and ran inside to find the man. He was walking around, I tapped him on the shoulder and said, "The bus is leaving, and we have to go now." He looked at me a bit confused, and I said, "Andalé! Andalé!!" Which means "hurry, hurry!" in Spanish. We both ran outside to catch the bus. I felt bad for the man. He obviously couldn't understand English very well, I thought.

Our next stop was in a city where the Hispanic man and I had a three-hour layover to catch the next bus. I sat on a chair and picked up a magazine that looked interesting to me. I really was hoping this guy wasn't going to come and sit by me. About fifteen minutes into my magazine, the curiosity got the best of him. He sat right next to me and started talking Spanish with a little broken English. Very hard for me to understand, but I was trying desperately. (Sherry told me there would be a day I'd wished I had taken the time to learn my native language. I didn't believe her at the time, but I was feeling it then.) We talked until our bus showed up—hours later. He told me that he was on his way to visit his brother in New York, and that he was coming from California.

It had been days since he had changed his clothes or bathed, and I could tell. I actually felt sorry for him because he didn't seem to have much. He told me that where he came from, he had been a wealthy man who owned cattle and land. He just didn't seem too secure to me, and he had to be at least twice my age. I had gotten on the bus first, so I chose a seat by the window on the right side of the bus about two-thirds of the way back. I sat down and he was right behind me and sat next to me. The bus was pretty full so I didn't mind. He seemed pretty nice and maybe I could learn Spanish from him. We talked for hours and then he tried to cross that line. He put his hand on my knee, and I politely said, "No" and I put his hand back on his own knee. He did it again, and I repeated the process again. He said, "Why?" I said, "Because we are only friends." Then he proceeded to try and explain to me that I was very pretty and that he wanted to marry me. I started laughing and said, "You are old enough to be my father." I told him. "I am only 18 and am not interested in getting married anytime soon." He told me he could make me happy with lots of children.

Again, I began to laugh and said, "Why would I possibly want children right now? I am on my way to college. I am not interested in getting married, having babies, or marrying you." I told him, "I am too young." He started to get frustrated with my independence and told me he was going to marry me and that he was going to follow me to school.

OK, I thought *enough is enough*. Now he is starting to frustrate me. I started to raise my voice and said, "No, you're not, it's a girls' dorm and men are not allowed in." He said, "Yes, I will come with you." At that point I was done with him. I just stopped talking to him completely and he got even more upset with me. He continued to babble on and on and I said nothing. He finally realized he wasn't getting a word out of me. He folded his arms and fell asleep. I prayed, *Oh my God, thank you so much, please get me out of this.*

I leaned against the window and fell asleep, too. We drove for many hours and I remember it was about 4:00 a.m. or so in the morning. I heard the bus driver say, "Baltimore. Baltimore, Maryland." I prayed, *Thank you God, now please help me leave without waking him.* I sat up and put one hand on the front seat and one hand on the back seat and jumped over him. I grabbed my things and did not look back. It was like a ton of bricks were lifted off me when I jumped off that bus.

Baltimore, Maryland. So this is what their bus stop looks like; pretty much just like Wisconsin's, I thought. I asked the attendant, "How do I get to Towson State University?" She said, "That bus doesn't come around 'till 8 a.m." "8 a.m.? What time is it now?" I asked. She said, "It's 4 a.m., Ma'am." Wow," I thought, *I can get some sleep.*

I found a nice chair in the corner and went to sleep. About 6:00 in the morning, it started to get very noisy and I started to listen to some of the conversations that were going on around me. I thought I might as well get up and get a cup of coffee. As I was walking over to the table, a nice-looking man confronted me. He said, "Hey pretty lady, so where you headed to?" I thought, "Oh no, here we go again." I couldn't help but think, *So, what is it about me all of a sudden? Am I advertising myself somehow?* Then it hit me. *It's got to be my shorts. They are too short for the city people; it must mean something here.*

This guy started babbling on and on about how he had this big yacht and that he was going to have this big party tomorrow night, and he wanted me to come. He asked me for my phone number. I told him I didn't have one and that I was from out of state and going to college for a summer course. I hadn't even been to my school yet, and that I didn't have anything on me that had the schools numbers. As he kept pressuring me for a number that I didn't have, a nice looking black police officer looked at me from across the room. I looked at him as if to say 'help'. He started to walk over toward us. He said, "Sir, are you waiting for a bus?" The man said, "No, I am just talking to this nice lady." The police officer said, "Well, you will have to leave, if you are not waiting for a bus." The man said, "Just give me one more minute." The police officer says, "Hurry up," and walked away. I thought 'oh no, don't go!' but he continued to walk away. So, I am again trying to explain that I do not have a phone number to give him. (We didn't have cell phones in the 80's.)

So, he gets this brilliant idea—he is going to give me his number. He says, "You have got to come; you will have so much fun." I am thinking in the back of my head, *What kind of man looks for women in a bus stop?* The police officer looks at me again and again, and I have the look of *help me!* The officer starts to walk toward us again, and I am jumping up and down inside, thinking, *Please get rid of this weirdo!* He says, "Sir, you have to leave… right now." "OK, I am leaving. Sweetie don't forget to call me," he says. I said, "I won't, thanks." As soon as he leaves, I turn to the officer and say, "Thank you so much, I didn't think he would ever leave." I asked him, "What kind of man tries to pick up women in a bus stop anyway?" He starts laughing and says, "I guess, *that* one!" I laugh and say, "Thanks again." He says, "No problem," and we part ways.

I had recently talked to a friend of mine named Lloyd who is from the city and knows a lot about city life. I told him about this bus station guy, and he informed me that pimps like to use bus stations to find their girls because lots of young college kids use the bus stops. I thought he was joking; I started laughing when he told me that, and I said, "Come on, really?" He wasn't laughing, and said, "No Helen, I am not joking, Think about it. There are a lot of young, good-looking, naive college girls who come in on the bus." He explained that the pimps take the girls out and treat them like queens for a few days. They give them the attention they weren't getting at home, buy them just about anything their hearts desire, then announce that the money is "out." To get more money for more fun, they ask if the girl wouldn't mind sleeping with his friend for a little extra cash to help out. She is feeling guilty because he has bought her so much and shown her such a good time. Many times the young girls agree to do this, and then the pimp has met his goal of making her feel indebted to him. "So… that's how it works?" I asked. Lloyd said, "Yes, and you really need to let these young girls know that in your book. It just may save one or two of them."

So here it is young ladies… "Beware of bus station pimps. They are alive and well and feeding on pretty, young, naïve, out-of-town guests!"

The bus finally shows up and I was more than ready to sit down. It doesn't seem long until I arrived at the school. I get off the bus alone, and have no clue where the office is located. As I start to walk towards the buildings, I realize that my arms are really starting to get tired of carrying the big suitcase. I am getting mad at myself for bringing so many things. I stop to rest and see a young man walking toward me, so I ask him, "Do you know where the office is?" He says, "Yes, it's on the other side of campus." He pointed. "You see that tall building? It's off to the left of that!" I say, "Thanks," and I start to pray, *OK, God, I really think my arms are going to fall off if I have to carry this suitcase any farther.*

I start walking and just then a man on a golf cart shows up behind me. He says, "Hello, would you like a ride?" I say, "Would I ever! Thank you so much!" "Where are you headed?" he asks. I tell him, "I need to get to the office, if you don't mind." "No problem," he says. As we are going, I can't help but think that I couldn't of walked this far with that heavy suitcase. The office really is on the other side of campus. He was such a nice guy; he offered to wait for me until I get out of the office to drive me to my dorm, which was still quite a ways away as well. I'm thinking, *God answered my prayer.*

We get to my dorm and it's a very tall building and I'm almost at the top. I get to my room and *Wow, what a view I have; it's beautiful!* At this time, it's almost 2:00 p.m. and I am getting very hungry and realize that I have no food or anything available for me. The dorm does have a kitchen I can use, but no pots, pans or dishes. I go downstairs and see very few people there. I ask a student walking by where the nearest grocery store is. He says, "Oh, it's about 5 blocks down the hill. Just follow that street and you can't miss it." That sounds pretty easy right? WRONG! I start walking and walking for what seems like an hour to me. I do find it, but it's way more than five blocks just down the hill. The hill happens to be very long and steep, and I am already exhausted and getting very hungry.

I remember buying a small frying pan, a dozen cans of soup, paper plates, plastic utensils, a 12-pack of Coke, two loaves of bread, a gallon of milk, and some lunch meat. I am sure I bought more, but those are the items I can remember. I wanted to buy enough to last me the whole time I was there. I get to the register and think, "Oh no! I forgot that I have to carry all of this home—up the hill of death!" I ask the cashier to double bag everything and asked him to put it all into two bags. He looks at me like I am a freak, and says, "I don't know Ma'am, I'll try." I say, "You have to, because that's the only way I can carry it." We managed to get it all in, but to use the word "heavy" would be an understatement.

As I am walking, I am thinking, 'Why did I buy so many heavy things?" I realize I wasn't thinking. I was just hungry and still am. It's now pushing 4:30 p.m. and to say the least, it has been a very long day! I have to stop five times to rest before I make it to my dorm room. I put everything away, but not before I made myself a sandwich and opened a coke. I realize how very tired I am, so I lie down to take a nap. I say a nap—but I didn't wake up until the next morning.

It is now Saturday morning and my classes are to start on Monday. Someone in the main office told me to expect a roommate to arrive sometime on Saturday. That prompted me to get out of bed as the sun was rising.

My roommate eventually showed up and she was a very nice young lady. Very quiet.

For the most part, school went by quickly, and I loved every minute of it. Two weeks in, my roommate told me that another student in her class asked her out on a date, but she was afraid to go alone. She had asked me if I would go on a double date with her, with a guy I never met. I thought, *no problem, it will get me out to see new things.* She really wanted to go, so I said, "Yes," and that next Saturday we got picked up. They seemed like two very nice Italian guys. We went to a local mall and then we split up—she went with her date and I went with mine. He took me to this oyster bar where he bought a dozen oysters on the half shells. I am a Yankee from Wisconsin and had never eaten an oyster before. In truth, I knew nothing about them except that they came from the ocean.

My date says, "Do you want some?" I said, "Sure." I am thinking, he ordered a dozen, so they must be good, right? He put it on a cracker and squirts some lemon juice on mine, I looked at him, then I looked at the oyster and it made me think: *this thing looks disgusting and I have to put it in my mouth.* I don't want to look like I'm afraid , so I throw it into my mouth and start chewing, and chewing and chewing. My eyes start to water a little as I am thinking, *this tastes raw.*

I ask, "Is this raw?' He says, "Yes, just swallow it." I have to put my hand over my mouth, so it doesn't come flying out. I swallowed as fast as I could before it's too late. *That was totally disgusting.* I now know I hate raw oysters! He says, "You are not supposed to chew them, just swallow." "What is the point?" I say, "They taste horrible!" He starts laughing and says, "They are supposed to be an aphrodisiac." *Great,* I think, *like young men really need that.*

We meet back up with the other couple in an hour or so. They drive us back to our dorm building and we say good night. I don't think my roommate and her date hit it off too well, because she made the comment to me that she thought that the whole date was a waste of her time. I didn't expect anything from my date, and he didn't expect anything from me either. I was just happy to get off campus. I thanked her for inviting me, and we never talked about that night again.

In my acting class, they had asked if any students would be interested in helping out with the play that was going to be performed by some of the older students. The play was *Fiddler on the Roof* and the dressing rooms needed help with some costume changes. I recruited my roommate because neither one of us had anything to do at night anyway. She got the women's dressing room and I got the men's. I had one very big challenge every night of the play. One cast member had to undress and redress in less than two minutes and that included lacing up his army boots. That was the biggest challenge of all of them, but it was fun to me. I am proud to say he never missed his queue, and always made it on stage in time. *Fiddler on the Roof* has since become one of my favorite plays. I appreciate the hard work involved—especially the Russian dance routines. It's just an all-around fun play.

Because we were involved with helping out with the play, we got asked to go to the cast party after it was all over. *Oh, boy how fun,* I thought, *I can't wait.* My roommate did not want to go because it was an overnighter, but I was not going to miss this one for anything. I got a ride with one of the members of the cast. I remember it was quite a ways out of town at her parent's house. It was a big house that was located on a very large piece of property. They had a huge spread of food and all the alcohol you could drink. I was an adult now and thought I could handle just about anything. So, I started off with a whiskey and Coke and went and got me a big ol' plate of food and sat down to enjoy myself. I talked with as many people as I recognized and enjoyed the music that was coming out of the big speakers. I was having a great time laughing and talking. Every time my glass was empty, I went and got me another one. *This is the life,* I thought. Everyone was having fun, and no one was arguing or fighting.

I'm guessing I had about five or six drinks when things started to go a little fuzzy for me. I started to feel a little tipsy and sick to my stomach. *Oh no!! This is not good, I am about to get sick,* I thought. *I saw a field with tall grass over the hill about 100 feet from the party.*

I started heading toward that field—all by myself. When I got back to the party about five minutes later, one of the cast members asked me if I was all right. I said, "Yes, but I'm not going to drink any more." He started laughing and said, "Good girl, that's how we learn." I was pretty uneasy on my feet and knew it. I walked into the house and found me a nice big beanbag to lie on. I curled up into a ball and fell asleep. My party was over, and I realized I had partied right past fun this time. The next morning was an eye opener, with a full breakfast for everyone who was there. I was not very hungry. I couldn't wait to get back to school and my room, where I stayed in bed most of that day.

I really don't remember my bus trip back to Wisconsin. It must have been uneventful, but I can tell you I am glad I took this trip. It opened my eyes to some life lessons I will never forget.

MORALS: It's OK if you drink soda or water during a party.
No one will ever know, and no one will appreciate it more than you.
Also, don't wear men's shorts in public, and…
Always be leery of good-looking men at bus stations.

17

MELISSA

A cheap shot at an eight-year-old.

There was a two-year time period in my life when I felt I was almost untouchable by the evils of the world we live in. After coming home to Wisconsin from Maryland, I had decided to go to Bible school. Besides, I thought Sherry and her husband were planning on moving up north, and I had to move on with my life. What safer place could there be than a Bible school? I know you're probably thinking, *what a goodie-two-shoes! Right?* Believe me when I say… God was calling me. No one goes to Bible school unless they have been called to. It's not something anyone would take lightly. It's a BIG step, no doubt, and I was about to jump in headfirst. We were supposed to get through the whole Bible in two years, and when finished, we could even go on to be a missionary, which I had planned to do—when I got there.

I was going to meet my friends Terri and Jeri at School. We had become very good friends and I knew their mom, dad, and whole family who always treated me as one of their own. A real family without all the drama going on! None of the brother or sisters was involved with drugs, alcohol, or anything else for that matter. I loved this family, and I believed they loved me.

Life in Bible school was almost too good to be true. We all got along and treated each other with respect. There was no fighting, arguing, or anger like I had seen in so many other places in my life. I really had two full years of joy and peace.

When I got there, I was placed in a room with three other ladies. Fern was from Venezuela, and was an MK (Missionary Kid). Ruth was a little person, with a very big heart and a love for kids. Cheryl, or Tweedy as we called her, was a descendent of Chief John Ross who led the Cherokee Indians. Then of course, there was me—a wild kid with a little chip on my shoulders who was learning fast to become humble. God was my lead, and I was learning to lean on Him without holding back.

There was one thing about this school, however, that I really hated. I had to wear a dress every day in class, but even that was becoming tolerable with God's help. Time went fast there, and I really enjoyed learning God's Word.

Every semester we had to switch churches, and I started going to a new church that seemed a little cold to me. There was a woman there who was about my age. I saw her talking to another lady and I could tell, just by her actions and without even talking to her, that she had been molested or abused in her past. I guess it's a sixth sense I picked up along the way. After talking to her a few weeks later, I found out that my hunch was right. She had been molested and had run away from home because of the pain.

While I was still part of this church, I heard that one of the families needed a baby-sitter for their three children. I love kids, and I surely could use the money. I took the job at their house after school once or twice a week. There were two boys ages ten and twelve and a little girl named Melissa who was eight. I had baby sat a few times already, so I was pretty comfortable with the house and family. Then one evening the mom picked me up and said, "Something is going on with Melissa, and we can't figure it out." I said, "What do you mean?" The mom said, "She is acting up. For example, her teacher called me last night and told me she caught Melissa cheating on a test. She also said Melissa was acting out in a way she had never seen before. She is getting mouthy and she gets angry easily." The mom said, "That's not like Melissa, but I have noticed some of this happening at home as well. Last week she got into a very big argument with her father in the car, and she lied to me and told me he slapped her face. I asked him and he said, No, he did not slap her. I am worried about her. It's just not like her to act like this." I said, "I will see if I can talk to her. Maybe she will tell me what's going on." I told her not to worry, "It's probably just a little phase she is going through."

That evening the oldest boy was not home because he was sleeping over at a friend's house. Her other brother was outside playing with a neighbor friend. Melissa was in the house listening to some music. It was a song called 1999 and I am thinking that most of you have heard it. Well, I knew it very well and knew it was not a good one because of the message it was sending.

Melissa started to sing it out loud. I said, "Melissa, do you know what you are singing?" She said "No, what?" I said, "Let me rewind this tape and I will explain it to you verse by verse." I started the song from the beginning and stopped it after every sentence. I repeated it back to her so she could understand it and then explained what the singer was actually saying. Half-way through the song, Melissa starts crying and says, "Someone is watching us." I said, "Melissa, no one is in the house but you and me." She said in a loud voice, "He's here, he's still here!" At this moment, 'I start to think to myself who could possibly be here? No one is in the house.' Then I felt it, and I thought 'she's right someone is in here.'

We had just had a class in school like a week ago about demonic spirits that were in some men and Jesus cast them into the swine and the swine ran into the river and drowned. I thought, 'How dare you, she is just an eight- year- old little girl. Melissa yells louder, "He is still here, please make him go away!" I said, "Melissa I am going to pray out loud for you and I want you to pray in your head with me OK.?" She nods her head yes. I said, "In the name of Jesus Christ, satan leave now!" Melissa, cried out loud with tears running down her face, "HE'S STILL HERE!!" Now I am getting mad. I can't help but think she's just a little girl. I start praying, "Lord, you say in your Word that your holy name will cast out demons, your name is that powerful. Lord, I'm calling upon you now, In the name of JESUS CHRIST, satan leave NOW!" I pounded my fist on the arm of the chair and it made a loud noise. I truly believed that, this time it worked. Melissa confirmed it by looking up at me and asked, "Why am I crying?" God had taken it so far from her that she didn't even know why she was crying.

A demonic spirit had oppressed her, and now I needed to find out how and where it came from. I started to ask her questions, "Melissa, have you ever played with a Ouji Board, Tarot Cards or Séances?" "No, I don't think so, but what are séances?" she asked. I said, "They are when a group of people get together and pray over a person or to a person and sometimes they say things all together." She looked at me with big wide-open eyes as if a light went off in her head. She said, "Yes, I think so. A week ago, mom and dad took us to some people's house we had never been to before. The lady there told us to "go down- stairs because the kids were all playing in the basement." So my brothers and I opened the basement door but the lights were off. We started to walk down the stairs and we could see a whole bunch of kids in the middle of the floor in a big circle. They had a lit candle sitting on top of a mirror in the middle of the circle, and they were all saying a lady's name."

(I have never repeated the lady's name when I tell this story to others I am not about to start now.) Melissa looked at me and said, "Helen, I saw her face." I said, "Melissa, what happened to you is called demonic oppression. It's when a demonic spirit in a sense sits on your shoulder and tells you to do bad things. Because you actually saw her face, you became the one it oppressed. It's OK. It's gone now. We just got rid of it in Jesus' name."

It seemed as though I had opened a floodgate. Melissa started telling me ev- erything that she had done that was bad for the past week. Like cheating on her test, and the argument between her and her dad in the car. But she was not lying, her dad did slap her face and I believed her. He lied to his wife and said he hadn't. Melissa and I talked for quite awhile and I prayed with her again that God would bless her and protect her throughout her life.

That evening after I put her brother and her to bed, I went into the living room and started to pray again for her and her whole family. I heard some noises coming from down the hallway. It sounded like someone was talking. I quietly walked down the hall and peeked into her brother's room, but he had already fallen asleep. I walked down the hall to Melissa's room and I saw her kneeling on the floor against her bed with her hands folded and her eyes shut. Melissa was praying. Wow, what an awesome sight I was witnessing! My heart was so filled with joy that I started to cry.

When I left that evening, I told her mother what had happened, but she didn't seem to believe what I was telling her. I guess it was a little overwhelming, but I do know she got her Melissa back.

I never saw Melissa again, but I still pray for her on the occasions when she comes to mind. I know God changed her life—as He did mine.

MORAL: Nothing is beneath the devil. Taking a cheap shot at an eight-year-old little girl is considered honorable to him. He has no boundaries and plays by no rules. By saying, the name of Jesus, you REALLY can cast out demon spirits. One more thing I know… I know I will see Melissa again some day.

18

DYSFUNCTIONAL MARRIAGE

You can't buy me.

I'm looking back 19-25 years ago, when I got out of Bible school and went with a friend of mine named Beth to work in a carnival. That's right, I was a "Carney!" We traveled around the United States for about six months selling food from those white concession stand trailers. We were living out of a moving truck. Part of it was a living quarters with a set of bunk beds, a small sink, and an itty -bitty shower. The space was so small that two people could barely pass in the walkway. It was my home, and I have to admit—a part of me really loved it.

After the six months were over, I moved to a little town just 20 minutes north of my hometown. I moved in with a friend of mine named Linda for a few months until I found an apartment of my own. I got a job driving a truck and found some new friends at a bar six blocks from my apartment. Life was good. I started playing softball on a local team and actually made the newspapers for being 8th in the League on its top-10 batting list.

I was single and free until one Valentine's night. My friend Tress, introduced me to her cousin and then… too many Bahama Mama's later, I am walking home with her cousin's arm around me. Neither one of us was safe to drive. He helped me get my shoes off then helped me to my bed. I was out like a light –still fully dressed. I realized this, as I was woken abruptly in the middle of the night from the urgent need to run to the bathroom. Yes, I had partied a little too much that night.

I got up the next morning thinking how dumb I was to drink myself right past fun AGAIN, and thanking God that nothing else had happened with my friend's cousin. I thought, *I will never hear the end of this one!*

Then, two days later, I got a phone call from my friend Tress, asking me what I thought of her cousin. I said, "He seems like a nice guy, why?" She said, "He invited me over to his house and was asking about you and wants your number." I said, "You didn't give it to him, did you?" She said, "We bet two out of three on a Backgammon game. I normally beat him, but this time I lost." I said, "Thanks a lot, woman!" She said, "Sorry, he is a nice guy. He just broke up with his fiancé a few months back."

Two days later, the phone rang and guess what? It was Tress' cousin. He asked to take me on a Harley ride. Oh, boy this is where all the fun starts.

Fast forward to one year later, February 7, 1988.

My mother-in-law is driving me to the hospital because my husband (yes, Tress' cousin) said he had to get to work and can't drive me. Yes, you read that right. I was pregnant about to give birth to his child, and he's got to go to work.

I had been having contractions all day, and now they were an hour apart and my doctor wanted me at the hospital ASAP. My mother-in-law stayed with me until she announced at 1:00 a.m. that she needs to head back home.

I am now in the hospital alone and up all night long. A very lonely feeling and a big pile of resentment suddenly hit me like a big ton of bricks. One thing you can bet about Helen is she is learning something from this situation in her life. There is a lot to say about Trust, Respect and Reliability in one another, and if it's not there, your relationship is in trouble and I knew it!

My baby's heartbeat starts racing, so my nurse calls my doctor. She then hooks me up to an I.V. because the doctor says I'm getting dehydrated. I am only two centimeters dilated, and my contractions are getting harder and longer. By early morning, my doctor is in my room and says, "I am afraid something is wrong, we are going to have to do a Cesarean Section on you. Please call your husband and tell him to get in here ASAP." So, I call my husband's work and apparently he had already left there around 2:00 a.m. or 3:00 a.m. in the morning.... I am not joking!

You must be wondering just as I was.... so where the heck is he? (I am using nice words..)

I called home, but no one answered the phone. So I called his parents, and his mother answers. (We lived on their property and she knew just about every single thing that went on at our house.) I asked her if her son was home. She said, "Yes, his car is in the driveway." I cannot explain in words the anger that instantly overwhelmed my whole body. I told her, "The doctor needs to perform a Cesarean within the hour, so please tell him to get in here ASAP!"

When I tell you I had trust issues with people, maybe you can partially understand? It seemed the more I got hurt, the closer I drew to God. A much safer gamble... He has NEVER failed me yet.

My husband shows up and I asked him what happened and why he didn't come to the hospital. He said that he got let out from work early, so he went home and played video games until 5:00 a.m. in the morning—then went to bed.

This was over 28 years ago, and I would be lying if I told you I understand why he did that. I held that inside myself for almost two years, before I brought it up to him again. Not good to harbor anger; it only destroys.

I can tell you—the damage was already done, and our marriage never got any better. In fact as time went on, the arguing and yelling accelerated to becoming down- right physical on both sides. I am not going to tell you it was all his fault, because by no means was it.

I was a very sick young lady who trusted no man. When you think about it, he never really had a shot with me—right out of the gate. Sure, I tried to love my husband and be as nurturing to our son as I could humanly muster, but I would be lying if I told you that I was a great wife and mother. I look back and see all kinds of ugliness, anger, lack of trust, fits of rage and dysfunction everywhere. I had no right, getting married or having a child for that matter.

I was nowhere close to being all right.

One afternoon, my husband and I were screaming at each other at the top of our lungs in the kitchen. We had pushed each other, and I ended up against the stove. When I pushed him back, I looked down and saw our son sitting on the floor playing with blocks and talking out loud, as if nothing was wrong. Something snapped in my head that very moment as if a light bulb had been turned on. I knew I needed out of this relationship, or our son was going to grow up with serious consequences. It hit me that it already might be too late.

I am not going to get into all the grueling details, but I will tell you that our marriage was very dysfunctional, and being a wife was not something I enjoyed.

Here is an example of where I was mentally. One day after work, he walked in the door with a dozen red roses in his hand. As he handed them to me with a smile on his face, I said to him, "You can't buy me." He looked at me with a very confused look on his face and said, "I will never buy you roses again." He never did.

I did not see it then... but I so get it now. Little Helen did not think she deserved roses, so she sabotaged the situation. Can you see the sickness in my thought process? I did not love myself... how can I possibly (truly) love another, or accept their love for me?

I couldn't. And I didn't.

You cannot put the cart before the horse and expect it to work or function properly. Again I repeat... I had no business getting pregnant or getting married when I did.

19

FLORIDA OR BUST

Life was better—but certainly not a bed of roses.

After finding a home to rent, we flew back to Wisconsin. Two weeks later, we sold my Harley to have money to move to Florida. We packed the moving truck, and my husband and another couple left on January 2, 1994, for Largo, Florida. I stayed back in Wisconsin with our son so we still could have an income and they could get settled and hopefully find work in Florida.

Almost two months later, my husband and I were talking on the phone. He told me, "Put your two-week notice in and drive down here." So I did as I was told, although very reluctantly, knowing that no one had a job in Florida and they were almost out of money. Knowing that not only was my Harley gone, but my whole investment is too, and no money is coming in. This was NOT sitting well with me at all, I am a bit upset over it, and my husband knows it.

My son and I arrived on a Wednesday, and a whole lot of questions came out of me that day. It seems the quick easy money they were expecting to make, was not going to happen. Millions of others moved down to Florida with the very same idea! Three adults were living in the house and not one of them had found a job in almost three month's time. I am not happy. I had just quit my good-paying job to come down here to find three people doing nothing. Not to mention that the couple owed us two months rent and food money by the time I got there.

Sunday rolls around, I get up, make a pot of coffee, grab my car keys off the counter, and head for the door. My husband says, "Where are you going?" I said, "I will be right back." I jumped in the car and ran to the gas station to buy the Sunday newspaper. Guess what's in the Sunday paper? Of course! The classifieds. I went through them with a fine-toothed comb. I found three companies that were hiring, and that really got me excited.

On Monday, dressed in business casual, I took off on a mission. I went first to the one I really wanted the most. I was there for almost three hours. I had three interviews with that company and landed a job that afternoon but, there was only one little problem—I couldn't start working for two weeks. The following day I found a local temp agency and began working for them until my permanent job started two weeks later.

Before I left Wisconsin, my Mother-in-law Loraine said to me, "Watch you be the first one to get a job." She knew me too well—she was right.

I am a Survivor; I will survive at all costs. You can't take away a Survivor's Securities and/or Purpose and expect them to be happy. There is no such thing as willing to settle in our vocabulary.

We are long-suffering people, but we always look for positive or forward motion. I have been known to throw what I have away to start all over again—that even includes my relationships. I will never tell you that this is a good quality. In fact, I think it is a personal flaw, and if I ever want another REAL relationship, I am going to have to fix that.

Webster's meaning of Survivor:
NOUN
a person who survives, esp. a person remaining alive after an event in which others have died : the sole survivor of the massacre.

My husband was the next one to find work. Then after a few weeks, the couple living with us followed suit. Life was better—but certainly not a bed of roses. Remember, I told you I wanted out of this relationship to save my son from a dysfunctional future? That promise to myself never left me.

My husband and I bought a house the following year, and a few months after, I moved out. You may be wondering, 'why, did I buy a house if I knew I was leaving my marriage?' The answer, 'I wanted to make sure our son had a home.' In my mind I was taking care of my own. Sounds crazy but that is how I roll. (I also continued to pay child support until my son graduated from High School.)

I moved in with a friend of mine named Kat from work. She was single, lived alone, and happened to be a lesbian. I know what you may be thinking. I know my husband believed there was something going on there, but he was wrong. Kat and I were, and still are, just friends who enjoy going on Harley rides from time to time with each other. I have stayed with her on a couple different occasions. We have always been just friends—nothing more, nothing less. She is one of those friends you don't need to talk to for months, but when you do, it's like, no time went by and everything is status quo.

After I moved out of the house we had just bought, I went to work and made an appointment with Shawn who is the main man in charge of the company I worked at. I wanted to see if I could switch shifts, from 3rd shift to 1st, so I would be able to have my son come live with me. That did not go over very well, because he said that is a childcare issue, which is not a good reason to switch shifts. My husband and I got divorced, with him taking primary custody of our son because I was on 3rd shift.

I found out after the divorce that if I had only gone to HR, I would have had the shift change granted to me. It is NOT a childcare issue, it was a custody issue. Big difference, they said.

Things would have turned out very different in my son's life, if I had only known this. Hindsight is 20/20. I believe things happen for a reason, and sometimes we never know what that reason is... it's just life.

Every day after work, (remember I am working 3rd shift, I get out of work in the morning), I would drive to the house, wake my son up, get him dressed, and feed him before taking him to school. My husband would rush around and leave the house as fast as he could. I guess he was trying to avoid me so the fighting wouldn't start. There never really was any closure between us. I left that marriage with only two carloads of things. I let him keep the rest.

I am thinking back on my life and what I had, and tears fill my eyes. I was so messed up inside, I harbored so much anger and feelings of betrayal; I trusted no one, not even my husband. I did not believe he truly loved me, and I thought we were playing house because we had a child. I was so miserably unhappy and confused with life. There was no way this marriage was going to last and I knew it. I wanted out in the worst way, and nothing was going to stop it. I never once considered his feelings or how I must have hurt him. It didn't really hit me until three or four years ago (over 15 years later) driving across Country in my truck. You know when you are alone with time to really think, all your past comes back at you from all directions. I was driving down the road and I just started wailing out loud for hours, so it seemed. I have made some major mistakes in my life and have hurt many along the way. I could beat myself up for it until I die, or I can learn from my mistakes and continue to carry on a better woman tomorrow... I choose the latter.

20

MENDING BROKEN GLASS

If negative things happened in my past that got me to react in negative ways presently, what is going to happen if I feed myself positive things in my future? The outcome is bound to change"
-Helen On Wheelz

I had just been to my very first visit with a counselor. Wow! What a mind freak. She was crazier than me. You can read a little about that in the chapter 'What to Look for in a Counselor'.

My second counselor's name was Linda, and I found her from a newspaper article I was reading. What a nice surprise, that was! Linda was very well seasoned as a counselor from what I could tell. She was a very pleasant person to talk to, but at the same time, she was very down to business—if you know what I mean. Exactly, what I was looking for at the time and also what I needed.

I had a lot of growing and learning to do, and I was very ready for this challenge. My marriage was falling apart very rapidly and I was very unhappy. Married with one child was not how I had envisioned my life at age 21. I would have fits of rage and terrible temper tantrums that I could not control. I felt trapped and very alone in this chaotic spin called life, and soon after meeting Linda, I realized that I really needed her help.

I was in her office telling her how I was so out of control with myself. Then something she said hit me like a brick. "Helen," she said, "you are sick." Wow, I thought, when we told each other that as kids, we actually thought it was funny! Well, this time I was not laughing. She was being serious, and I knew it.

I thought, "Wow, I am sick, I am really sick in the head." Not an easy one to swallow, but I definitely needed to understand the meaning of it and to find out why. "How do I fix myself?" I asked. She said, "Well, the good news is that you can, but it's going to take a lot of hard work on your part." I told her, "I'm ready to get started—right now!"

I had no idea the work that would be involved in mending broken glass. Here is a poem I wrote. I was trying to understand the cause of my pain.

The poem is about Abuse.

BROKEN GLASS

They call it love, but really to me,
It's nothing more than messed up insanity.
In this vicious world that we must live,
Everyone is taking and no one will give.
Who is guilty, who is to blame?
They should all hang their heads in shame.
This vicious cycle goes on and on,
Preying on innocent victims all along.
The hurt they cause, the pain they give,
Forever affects the lives we live.
Where did it start? How did it begin?
Was it with Adam and Eve in the garden?
The question is trivial, does it really matter,
Can you fix glass that has been shattered?
It can never be the same,
It can never be whole.
It can never be replaced,
When the original was stole.
Now we live our lives,
Trying to be new.
When the fact is,
We are tape, cement and glue.

-Helen On Wheelz -11/19/93

I know this sounds like a depressing poem and I guess at the time when I wrote it, it was kind of depressing for me as well. But writing is the only way I know how to rid the poisons, trapped inside of me. I don't see it as a negative poem; I just see it as 'my reality.' Something I HAD to face, or I guess, I could have chosen to continue living my dysfunctional life, but that is just not how I roll. I am nobody's victim, today, tomorrow or ever again.

So, I decided to finish this poem…as I see it now:

But wait one minute, you broken glass,
Has Jesus not died for our broken past?
Take another look, take the time to learn,
Dig deep inside, He can heal that burn.
Like a potter's wheel can change a hunk of mud,
Our Lord and Savior gave His precious blood.
No more pain, no more tape, cement or glue,
My Savior has made, my life anew.

-Helen On Wheelz -05/12/15

I added these few lines 22 years. later, after I grew up and learned about life and Christ's love for us. His love is a REAL Love.

It's how I see it now: Healed and Complete by the Grace of My Lord and Savior.

At that time, I didn't realize the long journey I was in for. Believe me, it seemed endless. I also knew that admitting to having a problem is the first step in fixing it. So, here I am thinking: I am sick in the head because of what has happened to me in my past, even though I was not in control of it and did not cause these happenings. It was sick people who affected me as I was growing up. That is the cause of my problem.

It's because of what they have done to me that has caused me to react and think wrongly as an adult. So in my mind I am thinking, *if negative things happened in my past that got me to react in negative ways presently, what is going to happen if I feed myself positive things in my future? The outcome is bound to change…right?*

But first, I needed to get to the bottom of this nightmare and face my demons. I knew I needed to start from the beginning of where it all started. It unfortunately began at about age five, when life was utter hell for me. So I started to dig, and I mean DEEP into myself and tried to remember all the nasty things I had tried to bury from my past. No one said this was going to be easy, and I knew that. I started by writing angry letters and then more letters that I wanted to send to the many who had hurt me.

(I go into depth in the chapter entitled *Meeting Little Helen*)

As I wrote these letters, memories started surfacing; things that I had pushed so deep, inside that I didn't even know they were there. I can't tell you the countless times I laid in my bed crying because I couldn't believe what was done to me. My little child's mind did not understand what was happening to me or why they were doing them. Now, as an adult, I am fighting mad!

When those memories surfaced of what happened and who actually did it., my reaction was, "Wow, OK, NOW… NOW you can say, I have a serious anger problem."

I could have killed someone at that moment, no joke. "How dare you, you son of a b... .," was my thought Wow, this is not an easy one to swallow even as an adult. I realized how very selfish people really are and it HURT!

Some of my offenders were my own flesh and blood. I do NOT count any of my family members above any of my TRUE friends. In my world, you EARN respect. It does not matter who you are. I have learned to trust NO ONE 100% except my Lord and Savior. We are all human, and humans make mistakes and sometimes say things they may not mean.

You see people can't hurt me anymore, unless I CHOOSE to let them. And, that goes for ANY category in my life.

John 2:24-25 (NIV)
But Jesus would not entrust himself to them, for he knew all people. He did not need any testimony about mankind, for he knew what was in each person.

Once I started to see the pile of garbage I was lying in from digging this all up, I realized something...

I see it.
I see it.... ALL!!
It's over!
I am not afraid of it anymore!

It is a big ugly monster, but I am looking it dead in the eyes and I am OK. Once I got to see it all, I then realized *I am now in control of this, it no longer controls me.* I am no longer afraid of my past because I just confronted it.... No more fear.

I know I am taking you briefly through all this, but in the chapter entitled 'Writing Them', I get into the battle and my actual writings that got me through it.

The title of this chapter is, Mending Broken Glass. Can you tell me how easy that is?

Better yet, tell me can you truly fix broken glass with tape, cement or glue... or any other compound for that matter... to make it new again? Think about it.... can you fix glass? Right now, knowing what you do, if I gave you a broken glass....could you fix it? Most of us would have to say, 'no'.

Why? We are not professional glass blowers and we haven't learned the art of making things out of glass. Things like the amount of heat used to get the glass pliable without actually over heating it to a liquid state? How much breath do I blow into it to form different shapes? What instruments do I use to bend the glass? I mean really, this could go on and on because I know NOTHING about glass blowing.

If I told you the quality of your future life depends on you fixing that broken glass, then would you be able to find a way to fix it? That is a question only you can answer. I guess you would have to see if it would be worth your time and effort... just as I did.

My answer to that question is "ABSOLUTELY... I'm worth it!" Just because I was raised in a dysfunctional home, doesn't mean I have to live in one forever. I live in America, I am free to choose, I am over 18 years old now, and I can be anything I put my mind to be, with no boundaries.

The only boundaries I have are the ones I put upon myself.

Unless you learn to break down the components of glass, you will never learn how to fix it, just as I had to do with my life. It's not easy, but trial and error will eventually bring you success in just about anything you do. Take the time to learn how to shape glass from someone who already knows how, and it is possible you could master it?

We are raised in a society where making mistakes is considered wrong. I do not see it that way. Some schools like to teach our children in that manner. Many parents discipline their children by saying, "No, don't say that," or "don't do that." Instead, we should be asking, "Why did you say that?" and "what did you learn from that?" I recently read a book entitled, The Whole-Brain Child by Drs. Daniel J Siegel and Tina Payne Bryson. These doctors believe that parents should "Connect and Redirect" when they are helping their children in stressful situations. I thought to myself, my gosh, no one ever connected with me by listening and understanding my situations, and they certainly never thought to redirect me to something positive. I mostly heard what was wrong. I remember nothing of connect and redirect. I had to figure this out for myself.

I needed to learn where my thoughts were coming from. Why I did it, said it, or liked doing it? And what I can do in order to correct it?

I needed to get to the REAL root of my problem, if I REALLY wanted to fix myself.

We are not perfect, we are only human and we should be learning from our mistakes. We make them because we haven't learned how not to... yet.

It may be something in our past that causes us to continue the same negative patterns. Until we clearly see that we have a problem, it may never be corrected. We're making the mistakes in vain. It's like trying to fix broken glass. Until I went outside the box to find help, I may never have found my answers and fixed them. I learned from my mistakes, and found out where I could improve as a person. I found a master in fixing me—I learned from Him and eventually mastered myself.

God was my first choice, because I believe that he knows me better than I know myself. Even better than that, HE is the one who MADE me in the beginning;. I thought 'I am going to the source. How Can I go wrong in that choice?
I didn't believe I could, so I took the gamble and bet on My God. Lets just say, I invested in Him with all I had. I also found myself a good counselor.

Take the time to learn who you really are, and invest in yourself. Read self-help books, attend seminars, listen to podcasts, turn on positive music, invest in a good counselor, find someone you can share with, explore different sports and hobbies. Focus on yourself. I can't tell you the amount of money and countless hours I have spent with the five counselors I saw throughout my life.

I can tell you, however, that I was, and still am, worth every penny and every second that I did invest in myself. I sent up countless hours of prayers.
Night after night I cried endless tears.
I invested in writing letters, poems, and endless other writings about myself....
I spent years trying to figure myself out.
I NEVER thought for one second, *am I worth all this?*
I knew I was worth everything, and I knew what my goal was....
My goal was to make myself well!

There is only ONE YOU and no matter what you experienced as a child, it doesn't matter.... you are an adult now.
Stand up!
Shake yourself off!
Be PROUD of who you are,
Go one-step at a time and focus on being a better you everyday.
You are very well worth it!... ... Believe it!
Not because I am telling you in this book but because... IT'S TRUE!
GOD DOESN'T MAKE JUNK.
YOU HAVE A PURPOSE.
FIND OUT WHAT THAT PURPOSE IS.
BECAUSE HE LOVES YOU,
SO MUCH MORE THAN YOU LOVE YOURSELF!

Did you know that if there were only one person in this world (you),
God would have sent His Son to die for only you? Believe it, it's TRUE!

WHY DID I WAIT?

"Lord forgive me" I heard her cry.
"They got this disease, they're all going to die"
I ran to her something seemed odd.
She looked at me and said, "Do you know God?"
I said, "Ma'am settle down, what are you trying to say?
You will be alright, it'll be OK"
She said, "NO, it's not me, don't you understand?"
Oh, Lord forgive me, there is so many... like sand."
"Lady, are you OK, do you want to sit down?"
"There is no time, I hear the angels and The Trumpet sound.
Oh God, I'm so sorry, why didn't I obey?
While I'm in heaven, they'll be in hell someday?"

-Helen On Wheelz 11/6/85

90%

They are lost, they are dying and bound for hell,
Their eyes are blind, cannot hear and trapped in a well.
What can I say Lord, What can I do?
What will open their eyes and bring them to you?
I am at a loss of words and I cry with concern."
But it's to my shame so many will burn.

-Helen On Wheelz

COR. 15:34
Awake to righteousness and sin not, for some have not the knowledge of God. I
speak this to your shame.

HIDDEN ROOM

The lights are out, so it's dark in here,
I sense loneliness, pain and lots of fear.
As I move along the cold damp wall,
I long to stand up, but I am too tall.
My head hits the ceiling, and I fall to the ground,
I yell for help, but there's no one around.
Where am I at? Where could I be?
It's not that hidden room, deep inside of me?
But I am afraid it is…But it's all right,
I'm much older now, and I have a BIC light.
As I reach into my pocket to pull out the light,
I hear a familiar sound, off into the night.
Is it possible? Can it really be?
Have I found the little girl trapped in me?
As I move to the corner wall,
I see her naked, curled in a ball.
Her face is dirty with tears falling down,
I am at awe, at what I have found.
This can't be real this can't be true,
All this time if I'd only knew.
I bend down to her, as she screams in fright,
I hand her my coat, as she begins to fight.
This cannot be, this cannot be true,
I just want to help, if she only knew.

-Helen On Wheelz 11/23/93

21

FOOTBALL

Playing football is in my blood from birth.

I have been watching football since I can remember. I am from Wisconsin. You can bet your sweet potatoes, I am a Packer fan… and proud of it. Every given Sunday, the football game was ALWAYS on at our house and everyone in the house was watching. My sister always made baked chicken and Uncle would come over and spend the day with us. We all knew what was in store for us on football Sundays, because they were always the same. A lot of yelling, and lots of food and drink. So watching, talking, playing football is in my blood from birth. Dudie and I actually each owned a set of Packer helmets and shoulder pads we used to play with in the front yard until my sister gave them away to some kids who came to visit at our house. Boy, was I mad and still don't understand why she did that. Would be nice to have that helmet for my collection today.

One afternoon I picked up the newspaper and found out that Tampa Bay has a woman's pro tackle football team. I called and found out that the season just ended. The owner told me to "hit the gym" because they would start practicing for the upcoming season in three months. He didn't have to tell me twice. I hit the gym running. By the beginning of the season, I was benching close to 200 pounds! The strongest girl on the field and playing center for the Tampa Bay Tempest.

Playing football was a total blast. Ladies, if any of you out there have ever thought about it? Do it before you get too old, it was more fun than ANY sport I'd ever played. I was 35 years old when I tried out for the Tampa Bay Tempest, but I loved every minute of it. I noticed my body didn't recover as fast as it use to when I was young, but it was so worth it to me just to get out and do it. I played two seasons for the Tampa Bay Tempest's, even played one game in the old Orange Bowl Stadium in Miami, Florida against the Miami Fury. We got our butt's handed too us but we didn't care.

I remember one of our players, Sam (we called her "Snow") got laid out on the field. She was on her back looking up in the stadium sky when one of the Miami Fury players came up to her, swaddled her body over Snow's, and yelled right in her face, "Your team sucks!" Snow looked up at her and said with a smile,

"So what… we're playing in the Orange Bowl." There were about five or six of us out there who heard her. We all busted out laughing as we walked up to the line. We seriously lost that game with a big fat "0" for our score, but it's a day none of us will ever forget.

I remember walking out of the locker room that night with my duffle bag in one hand and my shoulder pads and helmet in the other. It was very dark all the stadium lights were out and all I could see was a silhouette of someone standing in the middle of the field. I started walking towards her. It was "Jersey" one of our players who was standing on the 50 yard line talking on the phone. She had laid her equipment down next to her. I asked her "who you talking to?" She said, "Yoder" who was one of our teammates who couldn't make it to the game. In her other hand I noticed smoke. I looked at her and said, "What are you doing, are you crazy?" She started laughing and said, "Helen, you better take a drag. Who else could ever say they were standing on the 50 yard line in the Orange Bowl and took a drag." I looked at her and started laughing. I said, "Yeah, you're right, give me that." I don't smoke but I had to at that moment. It still makes me smile when I think about it.

At the end of the Tempest's third season (my second), there had been a lot of talk amongst the players about how the owners were mismanaging us. I had been thinking of starting my own football team and we were all in the locker room after a game when I noticed that all the owners and coaches were gone. I decided to let out my little secret to see what the team thought. I told them what I was thinking of doing, and they were all excited, and started yelling and encouraged me.

That night at the after game party, a few of us started talking about what to name the new team. Kimmie (wide receiver), one of our players, came up with the name Tampa Bay Fire Ants. We all started laughing. She was serious—she liked it—but all I could visualize was losing and the opposing team doing a stomp and twist action with their feet in unison as if they were killing ants. Another player said, "How about The Tampa Bay Exterminators? I liked the sound of it, but it wasn't quite right, and then BOOM… "I got it!" I said, "The Tampa Bay Terminators… that's it!" And that is how we got our name.

The next step for me was to get a logo created. I needed to find someone with the gift of design. Chris, one of the Tempest owners, told me her neighbor was a graphic artist. Her name was MJ, and she lived in Tampa. I met her at a bookstore to give her my ideas on what I was looking for. Within a week or two, MJ came up with three or four different designs. I thought I wanted a skull in the design, but she changed my mind when I saw her design of a silhouette of a female football player in a swirl. She tweaked it with a ponytail, some  bullet holes, and a less bulky body shape. Voilà! We had our beautiful Tampa Bay Terminators logo. Halfway through designing the logo, one of our players Lisa (wide receiver), ran into the wife of one of the players from the local Sheriff's football team called "The Posse" at a gas station. They started talking football, and the lady mentioned that she had a large quantity of some of the original old throwback uniforms from the old Buc's Creamsicle days. She wanted to know if our team needed any uniforms for practice and play. Wow, what a blessing to be offered the original old Buc's uniforms! When I went to pick them up, they filled up the entire back of my full- size pick up truck. We had more than enough to practice and play in.

We joined the IWFL (Independent Woman's Football League), and became an official team in the league of about 23 teams Nation Wide at that time. Life was good, and times were fun. We were actually the first team in Woman's Football history to own our very own Charter bus. We had our team logo on each side of the bus and our bus driver was Robert Standing Bear, a full-blooded American Indian. We had a lot of fun with him. I remember one night we were all coming home from an away game, and this old pick up truck pulled up next to us at a stop sign and started to beep its horn. Bear opened the door and the man yelled, "Are there women football players in there?" Bear said, "There sure are." The man said, "Can they show me their t*ts?" Bear yelled back, "Sorry sir, this time of night I'd like to keep them all to myself, " and he closed the door. The whole bus busted out laughing and yelled, "Yah, you go Bear!"

I remember another time: Bear went with us to an Atlanta game. We were playing the Atlanta Explosion. This was a very good team that was very hard to beat. We beat them our second season home and away. We were at their stadium waiting for all our players to come out of the locker room. Bear pulls out a bottle of something; he told me it was very old and he was waiting for a very special occasion to open it. He said, "This is it, the Tampa Bay Terminators beat the Atlanta Explosion for a shot at the playoffs. I want to share this bottle with all of you." We passed it around and every one of us drank from that bottle. What an awesome victory we all shared that day!

Our team did move on that season to the playoffs in Queens, New York to play the New York Sharks. It was the absolute toughest team in any league at that time. We lost that game, but we gave those old Buc's uniforms a few more years of playing time.

The Terminators 4th season (2006), was a complete disaster when I allowed my head coach to get too involved with the team's management side of the business. A mistake I believe I allowed, due to my trust in him. I thought this guy had the team's back. Instead, he got greedy and tried to destroy our team's future. This included purposely loosing games, forfeiting games, and convincing our players to end the season prematurely.

I blame a lot of our team's destruction on myself. By nature, I trust people. Usually it happens too quickly, which can end up giving away my heart and getting hurt. This one truly broke my spirit.

This team was my baby, my creation of a dream to eventually help little girls learn the art of the game. I had big plans for this team, but I also had a problem delegating because of either trusting too much or not trusting others enough. So my problems were many: those I didn't trust, those I trusted too much, and others I never could trust enough.

What effect did this experience have on Little Helen? This one was a tough one to swallow; it hurt very deep. Being betrayed by your right hand man, but isn't that how my whole life started from my childhood? Betrayal from some of my closest family... I guess I never thought of it like that before. I don't know... how many times is one supposed to pick themselves up before enough is enough? I had a friend tell me once that I was relentless. She said, "Helen, you have tried at so many businesses but you just keep trying."

Owning the team gave me a whole lot of confidence at being a leader. It also taught me to channel my anger a little better–something I can always use a little work on.

What did I learn about myself from beginning to end from this experience? I learned that it only hurts if you think it does. People will always be people; none can be trusted 100%. You've got to take everyone with a grain of salt and know that there is room for improvement (I include myself in that as well.) I don't enjoy football like I used to; it has been tarnished.

Without God in my life, I wouldn't truly enjoy life, nor would I still be here.

Every person who has experienced early sexual childhood trauma has the ability to... be stronger than your average person walking on this earth. It is in you, or you wouldn't be here right now. We are here because we fought like hell to still be here...period!!

In 2011 and 2012, I became a National Qualifier in Strongwoman.

Competition in Clearwater, Florida 2011.
Farmers Carry 350 lbs.

22

WHAT TO LOOK FOR IN A COUNSELOR

If you're internally not comfortable, then get out.

I am definitely no expert in finding a good counselor, but I do have some insight on what to look for and what to be aware of. To date, I have seen five different counselors in 25 plus years. That may seem like a lot, but it's not really. I lived in Wisconsin for the first 27 years of my life and saw two there. I then moved to Florida and am now seeing my 5th and final counselor. I can tell you that my first counselor was the worst one of them all. To be honest with you, I can't even remember her name, but I can tell you, I only saw her for one hour, and I never went back again.

For being the first counselor I had ever been to, I remember feeling very uncomfortable and on edge in her office. I felt she was asking me totally over the wall (crazy) questions. Questions that counselors I've had for months or years have never asked me. After telling her briefly what had happened to me in my childhood, I remember her saying to me, "Wow, that is the worst story I have ever heard."

I thought, *'Wow lady, you're more whacked than I am.'* I am no rocket scientist here, but I do know you don't tell someone that if you're the counselor. I could have been very mentally unstable or suicidal for that matter. Right at that point, I knew I would not be coming back, and she was wasting my time.

I actually was very reluctant to try another counselor, because I kept thinking, "What if they're all that whacked?" A negative thought I know, but I didn't hold it very long.

A few weeks later, I was reading a newspaper article about a counseling service and it actually looked very professional from what I read.

At that point, my home life with my husband was getting worse by the day, so I thought I would give it another try. That is when I found counselor # 2: Linda. Wow, what a nice surprise! A normal human being; someone I could really relate to. Someone with a sense of humor, which is very important to me because I like to laugh a lot. Life is too short not to. This person could actually help me grow and learn about myself. I really liked Linda. She allowed me to work hard on myself, without being afraid. She made it seem like it was no big deal that I had this Little Helen living inside of me. This is very important, because you want to connect with a counselor who really knows what they're doing. When I started to dig deep inside myself, it wasn't very pretty and I knew I needed professional help. In other words you don't want a brand new, fresh out of the books, counselor in the beginning. You want someone who is well seasoned and seems strong and secure to you. I don't mean physically, I mean mentally.

My advice to anyone looking to find a good counselor is this: If you're internally not comfortable, then get out. If you feel you can't trust or even feel safe with that person, you need to move on. Remember this person has got to represent a safe place for you to open up your little child. It's got to be someone whom you can trust when you are in a very vulnerable state of mind. You may go through a couple of counselors before you find the right one. That's alright. It's just very important you find *the right one* for you—and only you will know if it's right.

Listen, it's just like screening a babysitter, or trying to find a good business partner or a good teacher for your kids. All those qualities you hold true inside yourself are the same things you are looking for in your counselor. Remember your little child is just that… a little child.

You are looking to find someone to help you grow up that little person…that's it, you're looking for a good role model.

MALE OR FEMALE?

You may be asking: Do I find a male or female counselor? That is a question truthfully only you can answer. It is totally up to you, which one would feel more comfortable with. I prefer females; that's just my preference. I also feel that since I'm a woman, another woman has a better chance of understanding my feelings and all that I went through growing up. Even though she may have never gone through what I did, she may actually be able to relate to my feeling better than a male. A woman might also help me better understand (in a deeper way) how to get through it.

There is *no one answer fits all here.* Each individual is different. Your own prefer-ence is just that… your preference. Go with what YOU feel comfortable with, and that's the right answer for you. You may even want to try both.

NOW LETS TALK ATTRACTION

You know what I mean. If by chance you were molested as a child like I was or you have an addiction to porn, you really need to watch out for this. Some of you will know exactly what I mean by this, some of you will pretend you don't understand, and some of you actually won't.

Let me explain something to you. I was sexually molested at a very young age and that means, whether I want to admit it or not, my little child is sexually sick and will most likely be attracted to my counselor. This is why it is vitally important to find a counselor much stronger than yourself. If they are not very good looking that may help too. Just kidding....

I did have one counselor, Counselor # 3, who was considerably weaker than I in this area. I very well could've had a relationship outside the office. I chose not to go there, simply because I knew by doing so, it would jeopardize my emotional growth. You see when I chose to make myself well, I promised myself to do just that. It's bad enough to break a promise to someone else, but if I can't keep a promise to myself, where does it end? That is just asking for trouble.

I now control Little Helen. She no longer controls me. Believe me, that is VERY powerful. I just could not sabotage myself like that.

I chose to let counselor #3 go before it was too late, and I did something I would regret for the rest of my life.

It is important to know your limits, and to respect them as well as yourself. I try to think things out before I do them, and that way my mistakes are very limited. I look at the pros and cons before I make any major moves. I do that even more so today.

I am going to let you in on how I got through that situation without loosing it.

My counselor would say things that could be taken two ways. Things that would make me shake my head, and think, *did I hear that right?* So my first thought is, *is this person coming on to me, or am I imagining it?* This started happening more often. It kept going on from one visit to the next. I would not respond to these statements, I would either say nothing or change the subject (I am good at that... if need be.)

So one day I left the office and went to talk to a friend, one I trusted and knew would give me a straight honest answer, I said to my friend, "If someone said this to you..." and I told her the statement, "what would you think?" My friend said, "I would think the person was coming on to me." I said, "Well what about this?" and I told her another statement that was said to me, and again my friend said, "Yes, definitely." So now I have confirmation from someone other than myself. I know it's not me making this up. My professional counselor was officially playing head games with me and was interested in something more than just talking to me.

My next thought is, *Am I interested?* I guess that is a normal thought.

Well, this person is very attractive physically and smart intellectually, even gifted in an artsy sense, which intrigues me. So my answer to that is, *Yes.*

This is a VERY POWERFUL feeling—I must admit. Especially when you know the other person wants you. *I am interested.* THAT was the easy part of the situation.

Now this is how I came out smelling like a rose:

I think beyond the situation. In other words I play out the future in my mind, before I let it happen. I start asking myself questions about the future, like: *How many others has this person talked to like this? I can't be the first?*

What is my future if I pursue this; is it with myself or with them?

Do I think I have a future with them or do I want one?

Is this person good for me?

Do I want a one time thing, or a relationship?

What can I get out of this kind of relationship besides a fling?

Why would this person jeopardize our counseling relationship like this?

I think if this person is doing this, this is a weakness.

How did this person get this way?

All these questions start going through my head. Questions I must find answers to. So I start asking questions about this person and I find out that counselor #3 was molested at a very young age.

BIG FLASHING RED LIGHT!! STOP!!

I think… this is not good. Counselor #3 is in the same boat as me.

Even though there is a counseling degree between us. This is a very, very dangerous situation I do not want to be in.

My thought immediately is... *GET OUT OF THIS…NOW!!* This person is weaker than me, and needs more help than I can give and I refuse to be a sounding board. A relationship with someone like this would never last anyway. It also would be devastating to both of us in the long run, besides the fact that this is totally illegal and counselor #3 could lose their license to practice.

I decide to part ways. If you start building a relationship on a foundation that is not solid, your own stability will be jeopardized.

I had the power to control this person's future, or have a sexual relationship with them and say nothing. I chose to do none of the above, because ANY one of those decisions would also affect me.

I would be setting myself up for a fall, as well. I have chosen to make my Little Helen well, and with that comes a lot of responsibility. She has been let down most of her childhood. If not by the people closest to her, then by some of her friends. I just refused to let her be treated that way anymore, by me or anyone else.

Just because two people are attracted to each other does not mean they have to act on it. I do not believe we are animals—mammals, yes, but not animals. There are consequences to every decision we make in life. This is NO exception to that rule.

You cannot grow from someone who is weaker than you—they must be rock solid to be of any good to your little child.

Why, set yourself up for a fall? If you are standing on a chair and someone comes along and takes a hold of your hands, and you two start pulling on each other, guess who is going to win? The one lowest to the ground, the one on the bottom. You will most likely lose.

This is the same in real life situations. Surround yourself with strong mentally healthy people. Find people you want to be like. Give yourself something to shoot for. If we allow easy or weak people to surround our world, we are only inspired to be the same way; there is nothing to strive for. Here is a concept I tell people about finances.

If you want to be rich, then hang around rich people. If you want to be middle class, then hang around the middle class. If you want to be poor, then hang around the poor.

With the same concept, we become what we expose ourselves to.

You want to become mentally healthy? Then hang around mentally healthy people. Learn from them, learn how they think, see what they see. Do what they do, let them inspire you, strive to be strong like them, grow to be a more solid you.

YOU can be your best friend or your worst enemy. It all depends on WHO and WHAT you decide to expose yourself to!

IF YOU ARE ATTRACTED TO YOUR COUNSELOR

If you find yourself attracted to your counselor, don't think you must go out and find another one right away. If all the other qualities you are looking for are there, it can still work. You just need to really keep a close check on yourself, at all times.

Your little child is immature and may tend to say or do things that are a little inappropriate. Try to control your childish impulses and think twice before you speak.

Remember, as the adult you need to learn to discipline your little child. Teach him/her what is acceptable and what is not. Do not tell your counselor of your attraction.

(I say this with caution because counselor and client relationships have been known to happen all the time, and I see how easy this can go down. We are all human here and I feel if we take the temptation away by not exposing it to both sides, the risk factor lessons.)

The fact that you are aware of your attraction can help you keep yourself under control. It will also help you to know why you think some of the thoughts you do.

You must learn to control your thoughts, and know that they can never be pursued. Not only is it illegal, but also unethical. I believe it's a normal feeling due to the sexual immaturity we experienced in our early childhood. There is a good possibility that with time these feelings will lessen, and may go away for good. Understand that as your little child is growing up, how he/she thinks will start to change as well. As maturity and learning continue, so do your thoughts and feelings.

There are many types of attractions physical, sexual, mental, emotional, spiritual, intellectual and probably more. I think that any one of these could cause a possible problem if you let it. The key here is control, keep your relationship on an even healthy level at all times, to be safe.

You may find that throughout the day, your thoughts continue to go back to your conversations with your counselor. You may feel like this is part of the attraction you think you are feeling, but it is probably connection you are feeling. It's OK as long as the thoughts are not in a sexually unhealthy manner. Your little child is trying to grow and mature and it takes time. Things that you learn about yourself in your counseling sessions, or conversations you have had, will come back to you throughout the days ahead. This is OK, this has to happen in order for your little child to understand healthy conversation and learn about him/her self. For me, sometimes things that were said would play over and over again in my head, but I found that this was a process that was helping me grow mentally and helping me mature.

I will be straight-up honest with you, I needed a connection with every one of my counselors I had, or this counseling thing would not have worked for me. For me, this is a must-have when screening a counselor. I needed to connect with them in some way or I moved on. As I did with my first one who was just not right for me, that may have been part of the reason. I believe some type of connection must be there or you won't feel comfortable.

IF YOU ARE SEXUALLY ATTRACTED TO YOU

If the attraction is sexual and it's all you can think about, you
not being able to focus because of the distraction. When sexu.
your mind, to the point it's all you want, then it's time to let yo
(It's not that big of a deal, I did it with #3 counselor.) You need to
else who is healthy for your little child. This is especially crucial i
ning, when you start out seeing a counselor for the first time. You .
focused on making yourself well, without over- powering distractions

Again this book is not for the person that wants to stay in their dysfunctional life. I am writing to those that want to better themselves, and become healthier and stronger people. This is not an easy move or decision to make, but one very vital to your growth and well being.

As the adult, it's your job to protect your little child at all times. Know that only YOU have the power to make your little self well by the decisions you make every day, throughout your life. Be true to yourself, and you will find the right one for you.

IF YOU ARE A CHRISTIAN.

It's not a must, but my suggestion to you is to find a Christian counselor.

It may speed up your growth process, but most of all, they will understand you better.

People who are TRUE Christians believe that Jesus died on the cross for their sins. The others in the world may not understand us or get it, nor can they. Until they accept Him for themselves. The Bible states **we are not of this world** once The Holy Spirit enters us, we are of God.

23

ARE YOU A SETTLER OR PIONEER?

I have a hard time settling for just about anything.

I had a counseling session with Mona yesterday, and she asked me a question that I thought was very interesting. The question was "What is the difference between a Settler and a Pioneer?"

This question hit the "interesting mark," because we were talking about relationships.

Here's my answer:
"A settler is someone who settles for things. A pioneer is one who goes out and finds things."

I really didn't know that there was any special answer to this, so I just fired one off the top of my head!

Later, I looked them up in the Dictionary and here is what I found:

set•tle |setl|
verb 1. Bring to rest, come to rest 1: to place so as to stay.

pi•o•neer |pīə nir|
noun
a person who is among the first to explore or settle a new country or area.
• a person who is among the first to research and develop a new area of knowledge or activity

Just to add to that last thought, I believe a settler will also settle even if they're not happy. I see so many people at work who hate their jobs but won't do anything about finding anything better. They won't even look for change. They just "Thank God it's Friday every week." They are wishing their time in life away and settling by just staying put.

A pioneer, I think, is one who settles if it's right, but if things aren't right, they continue looking for something better. They may not leave what they have, but they still continue looking just incase they find something better. This can pertain to almost any aspect in life.

As I thought about it for a moment, I realized what she was trying to get to. Based on the topic we were talking about, it hit me hard, like a big light went off in my head. I think that most people are actually one or the other. I said, "Are you trying to tell me, I am not a settler but a pioneer?" She was taking a sip of water at that moment, and shook her head, "Yes." OK I am thinking, this is all starting to make sense to me now. Not only am I an entrepreneur, but now I'm a pioneer. This is a good thing, to me because it adds up to being a leader and not a follower.

It does have its price, however, just like anything else out there. It also means that I have a hard time settling for just about anything. Meaning—once I concur something, I have the drive to move on to something else. This can be good in a lot of cases, but not necessarily in personal relationships. Maybe it is good if the person you are with makes you a better person with them than you were by yourself.

Sometimes it's better to settle, but it's not so easy for a pioneer. Our drive is to continue marching on. Now that I have learned where the drive is coming from, I can learn to control it much better. It helps me keep an eye on my actions and motives.

I believe EVERYTHING we DO or SAY comes from somewhere in our past. If it's a mistake we are making, the only way to stop it from happening is to find out where it's coming from and why.

EXAMPLE:
Cheating on your spouse or loved one.
Find out your INNER core reason.
What is REALLY driving you to want to do this?
Be TOTALLY honest with yourself and your past.
Things you've seen or heard or been a part of.
Look at your fears, your history, and even your experiences.
Look at your self-esteem as well as what motivates you.
Look at WHY your married or date the person you are with in the first place and what has changed.

Being honest, when I was married to my husband seven years, I have to say I truly believe I had demonic spirits from my past that were oppressing me. I did not have a fighting chance to win them over on my own. I loved him and I loved our son the best way I knew how at the time... but it was NO WAY near where is should have been. I was still very sick and knew no better... I do NOW!

My relationship with Pat (lesbian partner, 17 years) also involved the spirits, but when push came to shove, I could not find that inner peace I craved which I needed so desperately to find.

I found it in my relationship with Christ...
I search NO MORE.

Be totally honest with yourself, or you may never find the REAL answers. Sometimes it's ugly and you may need a good counselor to help you through it, but until you face the REAL YOU in any situation you may never find the REAL answer to any of your problems.

I have found in my own experience that once I felt I was done with a relationship or a job situation, I went on to sabotage it by making a move to make it irreversible.

(I do not do this with my REAL friendships because they are not something I would throw away. They are gifts from God to me, or helpers in life's journey. I become a servant, and there is no limit. I will do whatever I can to help them.)

I mean jobs or someone I may be dating. If I get no benefit, or it's not right, I will not waste any more time. I end it. I feel life is just too short to settle with something that doesn't bring growth in my life.

There is a possibility you may have a spirit oppressing you as well.
With this one, finding a good Bible- based church and having them lay hands on you and praying the spirit out in Jesus' name can solve that problem. Once you find the reason(s), it can aid in helping you counteract your actions in your future. If we all let the adult in us control our actions, I don't think we'd have all the relationship problems in society as we do. The problem is our past DOES affect our future and because of that, it can change a person for the good or the bad. Only YOU can decide which way it will fall. If we learn to play our cards right and learn from our mistakes, we can all come out smelling like a rose.

For me, I am always checking my motives to see they are real and pure, not self-centered or wrong for whatever reason. Helping others comes very easy for me because I am a giver. I get more enjoyment from giving than receiving.

I enjoy putting a smile on someone's face—even a stranger. It seems very powerful to me to help others. Not in a greedy way, but in a loving and happy way. Like for that split second, that person and I looked eye to eye, and we were in a happy place together. I may never see that person again, but I know in my heart I got them to smile for just that moment together with me.

Smiling can be contagious and infectious, but so can many negative things like pouting and scowling and complaining... Let's just say I prefer smiling and genuinely meaning it.

I AM A PIONEER !!

24

BEING A LESBIAN

God's eyes are never closed. -Dr. C. Becker

I cannot answer for anyone other than myself, but I will tell you I personally DID choose to be with another woman.

This, for some reason, was very hard to write.

Maybe it's tough now because I am finally taking ownership of my own actions, but I will tell you, I know I was NOT ALONE in this.

Life is confusing enough. Some of you may agree with me when I say this, and some of you won't. All I can do is tell you MY experiences and be as honest as possible.

Being a lesbian is no picnic. I mean really... Who would like to live a life of outcast, fear, loneliness, hiding, shame and embarrassment? I knew I was gay in elementary school, I just did not act upon it.

Who craves to be outside of the majority? Who chooses a life where you shame your parents and your family?

Who wants a life where you're not in the normal range, not like others? How great is it when people look at you and wonder if you are a boy or girl as they did when I as a child?

I remember feeling like I don't belong; I was a total loner, very alienated. Trapped in a world I just did not fit in pretty much—anywhere... and now attracted to girls?

Who can I talk to about this unspeakable thing? What, are you crazy? Why would I even think about telling someone? People will think I am some freak or something.

All they would have to do is tell ONE person in grade school and my life is over! I just can't risk that. I come from a very small town.

Come on! REALLY? Who would desire this ridiculous life over normalcy?

These are some of the thoughts I went through growing up. So, I pushed these thoughts far, far away. And kept on living my life. And YES, I had lesbian thoughts way back in elementary school. Remember—I was molested at a very young age. In fact I remember being in a doghouse with one of my classmates in first or second grade.

No, we weren't petting the dog.

We all are quick to judge until we walk a mile in someone else's shoes and most of us never get that chance. But I used to be one of those Christians who thought that all homosexuals chose their lifestyle, and now I stand corrected.

My reason for telling this story is to get some of you to understand something: I DID NOT CHOOSE TO BE GAY... WELL, NOT TOTALLY.

I remember being married, watching TV when "those homosexuals" were getting married in a church. I was so disgusted with the whole thing, I said, to my husband, "How dare they corrupt God's church like that? God will judge them and they will all burn in hell some day."

I cannot tell you enough how God does not like us to judge others.
NONE of us has the right to judge ANYONE…. About ANYTHING!

Do you understand why I say this?

Let me put it this way.
"He who has sinned not, Please cast the 1st stone."

Romans 3:23
We all have sinned and come short of the glory of God."

Have you heard of the word, homophobic?
Yep, that was me.
I will admit it today…I feared "them."
People, I am only being totally honest here.
Why, did I fear them? Because I knew deep inside, I REALLY thought I was one.
I had those deep desires, those deep-seeded thoughts, and had been having them since my early childhood.

Wouldn't you know it, two years later, I am in the middle of leaving my husband because I was so unhappy. I waited one full month to think about things and found myself smack dab in the middle of a lesbian relationship.

Go ahead—guess where we got married five years later.
That's right, smack dab in the middle of a church.
A Lutheran church for that matter.

We got married by a Lutheran Pastor (not legally).

What nerve!
I am NOT trying to belittle this or make it of no importance, but don't we ALL sin EVERYDAY ?

This sin is no different than you looking at porn
or not forgiving someone,
or lying,
or gossiping,
or not honoring your Mother and Father,
or sexually lusting while married... or not married,
or stealing ANYTHING,
or sex before marriage,
and I could go on and on and on.
Sin is sin....period.
Just because you know someone else's sin, does not make it a worse sin than yours.
He tells us in His Word…. "DO NOT JUDGE."

Matthew 7:1
"Do not judge, or you too will be judged. For in the same way you judge others, you will be judges, and with the measure you use, it will be used to you."

What was I doing while sitting on my self righteous couch, telling my husband that God will judge all the homosexuals and some day they will all burn in hell? JUDGING!... AND SHAME ON ME!

NONE OF US ARE FREE FROM SIN…. NONE OF US... PERIOD!
No sin is greater or less than another, (except one, but I am not going to get into that).

I want to bring up something that just happened this last month as I am writing this. On 06/12/16 a terrorist went on a shooting spree in Orlando and shot and killed 49 people and wounded many others in a gay night club in Orlando. I am not going to get into the fact that this young man was battling his own feelings/demons.

A lot of talk came from some *so called* Christian churches about God punishing the gays. This is talk from people who DO NOT know the heart of God Almighty, *people talk*. Please do not judge God (on who or how God is) by what "Religious" people say.

People will always be people BUT that is ALL we will ever be... we are NOT God.

There is a big difference between a Born-Again-Christian who has committed his/her life and has a personal relationship with God, and a religious person.

They are NOT the same, not by a long shot.

God loves EVERY single person… ALL the same, ALL the time.
In fact He loves us just as much as He loves His Son Jesus, if you have accepted
Him as your Savior.
He loves us NOT any more and NOT any less.
We all sin and come short, most of us every single day.
Don't you EVER let ANYONE tell you different.
He shed His blood to pay for ALL our sins and
NOT just those that we do in private.

"God's eyes are never closed," as my friend Dr. C. Becker, always says and she
is right on.

God sees all and knows all, and He loves you right where you are, no matter
where you are.

He is not a respecter of persons…. man is. Man likes to put God in this little
itty bitty tiny box just because he memorized a few verses from The Holy Bible.

Do not be fooled people. God's love goes way beyond man's comprehension.
"God loves even the gays and trans-genders."

There I said it!
Now believe it!
Because it is ABSOLUTELY TRUE!

25

TAKE ME LORD

I feel so alone.

I finally admitted I was a lesbian at age 28. Today, the first part of this sentence is no longer correct. I am NOW looking inside the fishbowl from the outside, and "I am no longer a lesbian."

It should read: I finally gave in to fighting the demonic spirits that had been oppressing me since childhood and convincing me that I was a lesbian.

Go ahead and laugh! But let me tell you my story before you laugh too hard.

One year after moving to Florida and being very unhappy in my marriage, I moved out of the house and into my friend Kat's house. When she was gone on vacation, I was cat sitting. This was a move I don't believe I planned, but one I needed desperately at the time.

It's a story my friend Kat still laughs about when she tells her friends, "How Helen moved into her house while she was on vacation."

She called me to see how her cats were doing and while we where talking I said, "Guess where I am living? In your house, hope you don't mind."

The fact was—I couldn't stand living with my husband another day. I remember feeling so trapped being married, like I didn't belong there.

I needed out of this marriage, and oh by the way…. I think I am a lesbian.

Yet, I was a Christian. "How can this be?" I am thinking. I mean, I went to Bible school for two whole years. I just can't have this kind of testimony. I remember praying night after night, "Lord please take me, let me die in a car accident or something."

I cried countless nights, pleading with God. *No one will ever have to know that I am attracted to women—just please take me. I can't go down like this.* Night after night I prayed this prayer.

I actually got angry with God, "Why aren't you taking me? Please don't let me go down this path Lord, I am begging you! I can't hold on any longer, I am going to fall." The constant pull was so strong and so relentless. The little whispers in my head would just not stop. They just got stronger and louder. Night after night, I would get no answer from God. I remember feeling so scared and confused, wondering, *Why, are you letting me live?*

"WHY?"

"It would be so easy for you, and Lord you won't have to feel embarrassed of me. No one would have to know."

Day after day, I would get no answer from Him. This was something I was not used to; we used to be so close to one another, and now I feel so alone.

"Why?"

"Why is this happening to me?"

"Why can't I fight this, Lord?"

"I fought drugs in high school, alcohol in my early 20's, even the devil with your help.

But I can't seem to fight this?"

"Why Lord… why are you allowing this?" PLEASE answer me."

"PLEASE, I AM BEGGING YOU!"

"Lord, You don't have to let this happen."

"Please, take me home…. I am ready." I have given you permission to stop this, but you won't do it. I so don't understand what is happening in my life… are you punishing me for something?"

It seemed that no matter what I would ask, I would get no answer.

Time went on and I left my husband and was able to keep living with Kat. After a month, I was in a relationship with a woman, and I remember praying. "Lord… do you still love me?" Of course I got no response; it seemed as though I was in doubt of His love.

I guess at the time I was…. ye of little faith.

26

GOD LOVES GAY PEOPLE

Tell Helen I love her.

About two weeks later, after praying that prayer, my supervisor at work (Kevin) came up to me at the end of our shift. He said, "Helen I have to tell you something. You are going to think I am crazy, but I just have to tell you."

(Just to let you know, Kevin was a Christian and he knew I was, too. He also is the person who introduced me to the church I am attending today.)

He said, "Helen, last night I was in bed praying to God." I said, "Lord, I am open to your will, and whatever you need from me, I am your servant—use me." I went to sleep and at 4:23 a.m. I sat up in bed and heard God say, "Tell Helen I love her." I said, "What, Lord"? And again he said, "Tell Helen I love her."

"Helen, I know you probably think I am crazy right now, and I was stressing all day. Thinking when would be a good time to tell you, and now it's the end of our shift. I had no choice but to come out and tell you before you left."

A tear ran down my face, as I said, "Kevin, two weeks ago I prayed to God and asked Him, *Lord, do you still love me?* Thank you so much, I really needed to hear that."

For those of you out there who think all gays, lesbians, and trans-genders actually CHOOSE their life style: I am here to tell you, I believe I am a product of my past. I can't speak for anyone else out there but myself. I can tell you, I fought HARD and even chose death over THIS being a part of my life's journey. Being a lesbian is not something I planned. It's something very understandable because of my sexually abused/molested past. I could not figure it out for most of my life, but I see it all clearly now. I had been in a relationship with Pat (my lesbian partner) for over 17 years. That's almost double the amount of time your average marriages last today in America.

For part of my life, I thought I was born this way. That is what a majority of the gay/transgender community believes. To be totally honest, I think we all are born in original sin or born as carnal/natural man.

Today, being totally honest with myself, I must take full responsibility over my own actions. I DID CHOOSE to give into my flesh and the demons that were oppressing me from my childhood.

The problem is, I had gone to bible school for two years and studied The Word intensely. The real fact is, I am held accountable for my knowledge before God.

My spirit fought to flee from this lifestyle for many years, but my flesh ran to it whole-heartedly.

All the past pain and anger toward men made it so easy to run this way. It was much easier than facing my demons and shortcomings. I was not wanting to deal with my past for 17 years of my life.

It was only when I looked inside myself did I realize how REALLY unhappy I was.

IT'S BEEN I

Lord, you have always been there when I've needed you,
It's been I- that has moved away from you.
Lord, you have always heard me when I've cried out to you,
It's been I- that has stopped listening to your voice.
Lord, you have always welcomed me with open arms,
It's been I- that has pushed away your strong embrace.
Lord, you have always loved me with an agape love,
It's been I- that's not willing to love myself.
Lord, you have always given me a peace that exceeds understanding,
It's been I- that has not allowed that peace to flow.
Lord, you have always given me a joy beyond comprehension,
It's been I- that has not allowed the joy to fill my soul.
It's been I Lord... .. all this time.
It's been I.

-Helen On Wheelz 01/07/2012

Some random thoughts:
My heart cries out for you Lord,
I want only your will in my life.
Why, is it sometimes so hard to be obedient?
To the one that gave His all for me.

TAKE ME OUT OF ME

Take me out of me, O Lord
In all that I say.
Take me out of me, O Lord,
In all that I do.
Take me out of me, O Lord,
In all that I am.
Take me out of me, O Lord,
And make me more like you.

I surrender my whole being,
To serve in this great fight.
To lead by example,
And to walk in your light.

A daughter in your image,
And heir to your thrown.
Surrounded by your love,
How can I go wrong?

Protected in Jesus Name,
How precious is THAT Blood.
I profess your Great Deity,
And all that is good.

Take me out of me, O Lord,
In all that I say,
Take me out of me, O Lord,
In all that I do.
Take me out of me, O Lord,
In all that I am.
Take me out of me, O Lord,
And make me more like you.

-Helen On Wheelz 12/26/2013

This poem took over five years to complete.

27

MY SOUL MATE?

We got along, I loved her.

My husband and I were separated for one month before I realized I was not turning back. I was happier living with my friend Kat, and I was ready to move on with my life. I know this sounds so selfish and I will be the first to tell you... IT IS. I will also still stand on the fact that I did not belong in a marriage or with child in the mental condition I was in. Those are not easy words to put on paper, "Mental Condition," but I am only being totally honest with you the reader, and myself. I was a very "mentally sick" young wife and mother (those two words hurt, too) but so true. The only problem is, I didn't know how sick I was. I was just flying by the seat of my pants and failing miserably. Like a wrecking ball going through a building, destroying everything in sight with no regard to life...that was me!

The only way I knew was "forward." That is the direction in which I moved. One month after I moved out of the house, a group of us went out drinking after work and then out for breakfast. I was on a mission to find a local paper that I knew had (personal) classified ads.

As I am writing this, I am in total awe at how this is REALLY going to look to the reader. I feel like such a piece of sh*t, but it is the truth and is my past. I cannot change it, but can only learn from it. I am NOT the same person I once was... THANK YOU GOD!!

I also just realized, "I do not deserve to be with another person as long as I live on this earth." I do not know my future, but I so see my pitiful past.

"Wrecking Ball" is the only word I can relate to, looking back.

If I never marry again, I have to say... I GET IT AND TOTALLY UNDERSTAND!

So as we are leaving the restaurant my friend Kat says, "Hey Helen, there is the paper with the classified ads you are looking for." I am so excited, as I grab one and head home.

That night, I looked through the ads and I circled a couple, but put a star next to one of the ads and went to bed. I did not tell you the ads I am looking through

are titled,
"WOMAN SEEKING WOMAN"
Did I just freak you out?
Are you surprised?
You shouldn't be.
Do you remember?
I have been sexually abused, repeatedly by boys/men.
Are you asking, "What does that have to do with it?"
Absolutely EVERYTHING!

I will get into all that in another chapter, I need to try and stay on track with my story.

The next morning, Kat has some errands to run so I was home alone. I went through every one of those ads again and went back to the starred one. I was feeling quite brave, so I picked up the phone and called. It was a voice recording of a person named Pat and she sounded very nice, actually too nice. I left her a brief message with my phone number, but I was nervous as all get out. I remember the adrenaline rush in doing that kind of thing, and it was just plain wild.

My counselor Mona, told me I need to be careful because I am a bit of an adrenaline junkie.

I did not know Mona during this time in my life, but looking back I can see why people cheat. What a Rush!

I am by no means approving of cheating but am now very aware and understanding how the devil makes it so appealing to us humans. We are such simple-minded creatures. If you throw the ball, we will bring it back.

So the waiting game was on as I hung up the phone and went on with my day. The next morning, Kat and I went to church, and when we got home there was a message from this Pat on the answering machine. She had left me her phone number. To tell you I was excited would be an understatement! I was jumping out of my skin. I was so nervous, but I called her right back. She did not answer, so I left another message on her answering machine, telling her approximately when I would be home that day.

Later that day, the phone rang. Kat and I looked at each other, and we knew that was her. I said to Kat, "You answer it," and started laughing as I walked over to the phone, took a deep breath, picked it up, and said, "Hello," as this sweet little voice said, "This is Pat, I am looking for Helen." I said, "Well Hello, Pat, this is Helen. How are you?"

That night, July 10th, I had a softball game and that is where we met for the first time. I can tell you it was the worst game I have ever played in my entire life. I played 1st base on a co-ed team and could not catch, throw, or bat that night. Kat told Pat, "I don't know what is wrong with her, she never plays this bad." I was totally out of my head that night. I could not concentrate and lost all self-control. I missed the ball when it was thrown to me, and when I did get it, I threw it over the pitcher's head. I was absolutely horrible!

Even my teammate, Chuck, who was pitching, looked at me with dismay as I just shook my head.

Remember, I told you I was in the town newspaper because I made the top 10 batting averages list for the league a couple years prior? Well, none of that mattered that night, I was head over heels in love at first site with this Pat. I could not wait to be done with that game and I love softball a lot. I wanted off that field in the worst way.

When the game was over, I rode with Pat back to Kat's place, took a quick shower, and was officially on my first date. We stopped at a restaurant for dinner and that is where she asked me the profound question. "Do spirits have genders?" She said, "I mean, if you take away our physical bodies, are our spirits male and female?"

I had gone to Bible school for two years and do not ever remember coming across an answer for that. "A very good question, I said. I really do not know." Then she said, "Then why can't two spirits be in love?"

Was she talking about herself and me?

Was she feeling what I was feeling about her already?

Was this the one my soul craved to find?

Have I just found my key to heaven on earth?

Is this the one God has send me?

I was jumping inside with so many questions and EVERYTHING was just so right in so many ways....or so I thought.

We finished eating and drove to John's Pass for a sunset walk on the beach. I poured my guts out that night, confessing everything. One thing I am not, is a liar. I told her everything and hoped for the best.

I do not believe lying is ever the answer. If she would have walked away that night because of the truth, I would have accepted that and carried on with my life. I am no angel and neither was she, but I knew one thing for sure that night. I was already in love with her spirit and I was in way over my head. She was not only drop-dead gorgeous, standing 5' 2" and 105 pounds, but her tranquil spirit totally captivated me.

I was in trouble—deep trouble—and I knew it.

My husband did not know it, but he had already met his future wife. Every evening after work, he would pick up our son from (after school) daycare. There was a lady there who had her eye on him. She found out from our son that he was separated and she started to pursue him.

How do I know this? Because a friend of mine had a premonition and told me that 'he has already found his future wife but he doesn't know it yet.' She told me that they would eventually get married and they would be together for the rest of their lives.

She also told me that I would find someone and that we would be together for a long time.

I don't know... is 17 years a long time?

I am single now... as I am writing this book. My soon to be ex-husband did marry her, and they are still married today.

To be honest, my relationship with Pat was good, and I truly believe we would still be together today if I would have settled. We did not argue or fight like most. We got along, I loved her, and I know she loved me. I trusted her and she trusted me. We had good jobs, a house, transportation, and I even had a Harley. We went on vacations every year and life was good.

But it was not enough for me.
I was STILL searching for SOMETHING.

Something I just could not find in her.

Something I could not or would not live without.

Something I could not settle in life without.

Something I needed in my core being to truly find TOTAL peace inside myself. THIS really had noth-ing to do with Pat—it was all about me.
My journey.
My hope.
My prayer to find the ONE THING that would fill the emptiness that I so craved to fill.

Would this empty feeling ever subside?
What is it I am REALLY looking for?

After seven years with my husband and leaving him, then another 17 years with Pat, and I have (just about) everything your average person could possibly want or need.

But did I...?
So why do I still feel so empty?
What is wrong with me?
What is it I am so needing in this life?
What is it I am REALLY missing?
I cannot answer ANY of these questions.
But my search is not over.
I cannot settle without finding the answer.
Half of my life is over and I have not found the key to total peace in my life.
I need to move on—but how?
How do I leave someone who adores me and so relies on me?
How do I tell her she is not enough?
How do I break her heart?
How do I get out?

I am crying as I am writing this, because she was 'My Baby'--my safe place.
My rock when no one else cared,
She was my world...
but she was not enough... to keep me.
The word, 'wrecking ball' is back.

What is it I am craving?
Would a man cure this insatiable thing, I am feeling?
My desires go beyond what she can fulfill.
I'm wanting to be treated in a very rough and aggressive way.
Where is this coming from?
What is wrong with me?

28

IMAGO

Give it a try.

I am having a tough time with this chapter because I don't know where to start. I was in a lesbian relationship that was failing. It was not failing because we didn't get along or because we didn't love each other. It was because I could not find total peace inside myself. I am not one to settle for being happy... NO, I want it all. I want ALL that life has to offer me, and I was not willing to accept almost or even second best.

I have grown so much mentally and emotionally in the past few years. This last lesson has been the hardest for me in the relationship area as well as my self-esteem. I could easily feel shame for being in a lesbian relationship for so long, but I won't allow that. It's a life- lesson learned, and that is how I see it. It doesn't pay to beat myself up over something; I learned to make me a better person in the long run.

After all, isn't that why we are all here?

I was at the point in my 17-year relationship where leaning forward was all I had to do to fall off the cliff and be out of this relationship for good. I saw no other option but to jump ship and move on with my life when I found this *save all* weekend class.

I sent a text to my counselor, Mona, to see if she had ever heard of this thing called "Imago." She texted me back, "Yes, very good" and commented we should "give it a try."

As a last ditch effort, I gave my partner an ultimatum, "We either go to this, or I am done with us for good." Before I knew it, the decision was made—we were going to the class. I really didn't have that much faith in this, but I thought 17 years is an awful lot to throw away. We've got to at least try.

The class was ten hours per day, and it ran Saturday and Sunday. Can two people's lives actually change in that amount of time in one room?

I was about to find out.

We both went I think, in desperation more than anything—at least for me it was.

When we got there, only one other couple was there. It was actually very nice and private. The counselor's name was Lin, and she is this tiny little lady with this huge sense of being about her. I actually felt quite safe and relaxed in the room. I was hoping for a miracle or a new beginning, or maybe a quick fix. I had mixed feeling, as well as feeling drained and tired of the relationship world I was in. Here is my thought: If it doesn't work, I get out. Simple.

I then at least can't say, *We didn't try...* right?

The class starts, and we introduce ourselves. Within five minutes, Lin had us close our eyes and imagine a few things as she talks us through it. We opened our eyes, and I am called on first to speak. The question was asked, "Why are you here?"

I find out that my whole purpose for living is based around writing this book and helping others. I need to keep going and make sure I finish it and get it out there to those in need.

(I realize today, not once did I mention my partner.)

My partner is next, and what I hear instantly brings me to tears. That's right—I am crying within 15 minutes of being in this class.

(Well, what can I say? When it comes to feelings I am very in tune with mine as an adult, not afraid of them anymore.)

The words that come out of my partner's mouth, literally take my breath away and I instantly see the depth, the commitment of my partner's life entwined with mine. This is an unbelievable realization to me. I turned and looked at my partner and said, with tears in my eyes, "You're here for me?"

She looked at me with stiff lips and shook her head, yes. Tears ran down my face, and I said, "I didn't know." I am overwhelmed with so many thoughts and feelings, I have to force myself to stop thinking about it, so the next couple can take their turn.

In that first 15 minutes of that class, I knew I was ALL in. This is the person I have chosen to be with until the day I am able to move on. Her deep love and commitment toward me is elating. I never was able to accept this from my husband, because I was violated by males at such a young age and hadn't dealt with it.

I know, looking back, that I never had feelings this strong for him. This feels so Real and True in its purest sense... but now, years later...I see it.

She was a NEED at the time.

There is a song they played by Roberta Flack in that class that stops me in my tracks and instant tears fill my eyes… STILL TODAY. I believe, REAL love for another human being NEVER dies, but it doesn't mean we were right for each other.

Then, is this relationship RIGHT for me? Back then because of the severe damage I experience as a child, I can say she fulfilled a deep-seated need.

• Today, I found an anonymous saying that fits this perfectly: "You stop attracting certain people when you heal the parts of you that once needed them."

• Was this God's plan for me?
I believe the answer is, *No*. I believe He is all-knowing and knew my footsteps before my existence. But I chose to walk this way… due to my broken past and pains.

• Does He like it?
No, I believe He doesn't like anything we do that is not Holy.

One of the class exercises was taking us each back to our little child. (When I tell you that, I mean it the same way I have taken myself back to write some of the chapters in this book.) When that happened with my partner, I truly could not believe what I saw. It was like I was looking at the two or three-year-old little girl she once was. So innocent, scared and alone… she opened her whole self to me that day in the truest form I have ever seen in a human. That takes TOTAL trust and PURE love to bear one's soul to another in that manner. I know OUR LOVE was real, in it's purest sense. In fact, I believe REAL LOVE NEVER DIES.

Do I still love her today? Of course!! I would die for her if need be, in a heartbeat! Then in saying that, there isn't a TRUE friend that I have today that I wouldn't do the same thing for.

THAT IS TRUE LOVE!

Did not Christ die for us all, to save us from our own sin? Did He not give all?

So with THAT being said, I need to get down to… WHY? Why did our relationship end if we were so in love? Oh, an Excellent question!

Here is what I know: I personally could not find REAL PEACE, or TRANQUILITY within myself or my partner. This thing that I am looking for does not come from the world. It ONLY comes from GOD (I didn't know that then.) It's that deep-seeded hunger or need we feel deep in the core of our being. The drive for real peace and contentment no human can give. It's beyond my wildest dreams but I knew it existed… I just needed to find it.

I also believe most people truly do not have it. In fact, I think we keep ourselves so busy in life or crutched in addictions, we simply don't pay attention to that NEED we have deep down inside. We know there is emptiness or deep-seeded pain inside, but we cover it up with things. Things to help us NOT feel or acknowledge our pain. But we ALL know it's missing.... and we keep searching and searching and searching.

The problem for me was, being in this kind of relationship separated me from God, and blocked me from that inner peace I so desperately wanted and I knew I was missing. It's that deep in your core loneliness or emptiness. I know you know what I am talking about, because we are all born with it and it never goes away until we meet Jesus.

Matthew 6:33
Seek first The Kingdom of God and His Righteousness, and all things will be given to you.

Romans 8:5-8
"Those who live according to the sinful nature, have their mind set on what that nature desires; but those who live in accordance with The Spirit have their minds set on what the Spirit desires. The mind of sinful man is death but the mind controlled by the Spirit is life and peace; the sinful mind is hostile to God. It does not submit to God's law, nor can it do so. Those controlled by the sinful nature can not please God."

I have a poem I received a few years ago from my counselor. She asked me if I would put it in my book. She told me she received it from an 11-year old little girl who had been abused. She wanted it put in my book anonymously.

I think it fits perfectly right here.

WOUND

A wound has burst open inside me.
Little did I know,
That I tried to seal up this Wound many years ago.
I tried to stitch it closed,
To hide it from the world, But then, Out of the Blue,
Something "New"
Opened up that wound that I tried to seal up many
Years ago.
Now I am Mending, Mending The Wound
Dealing With the pain
From that Wound. Sealing it up, Once again
To bury deep down in my soul.
Only to have it bust once more.
Trying to stitch closed, to hide from the world
The pain from that Wound

That burst open, many years ago. That hurt me deeply,
And though it pains me so,
I must forget. The Wound that burst open many,
Many painful years ago.

-Anonymous (11 year old girl)

This poem is full of pain and it's destruction and constant reminder in one's life. This pain never goes away without a knowledge and relationship with the ONLY one who died for it.

29

GETTING OUT

Something was missing.

I need help, I need to talk to someone who knows me and, at this moment in time, there is only one person I would trust with these thoughts. It's my awesome counselor who I used to go to a few years back.

Her name is Lorraine and I need to see her ASAP.

I go in search of my counselor's number. As I am digging through my old phone numbers, I find her name 'LORRAINE'. I give her a call, but when I hear the voice on the other end, it is not hers; I do not recognize this person. She says her name is Mona. I ask her, "Can I please speak to Lorraine?" and she tells me, "Lorraine is no longer living in the area." *What?* I am very puzzled and a bit upset. Lorraine was my lifeline to dealing with any problem that Pat and I encountered in our relationship.

If I see a problem, I fix it. That is no joke and it pertains to ANYTHING in my life.

Now she (my lifeline) is gone without any warning. Mona says she has taken all of Lorraine's clients.

I don't know about this, *what a shot in the dark...* I am thinking. But I agree to meet with her, although I am very reluctant.

I arrive at Lorraine's old office a few minutes early. As I am sitting in the waiting room, I hear this eruptive, contagious laughing. As the door opens, two people walk out, and they say their goodbyes in a very caring and loving way. I can tell they both are being very sincere, and in my mind this is a very good sign.

I am already smiling as this beautiful, tall, slender, curly red headed, dressed-to-the-nines lady, full of energy walks out from behind the door frame. She has this big smile on her face and she extends her hand out to shake mine.
She says, "Hi, I am Mona, and you are... Helen?" I say, "I am. Nice to meet you, Mona," as I shake her hand and we walk down the hallway to a room I am very familiar with.

The first session with a new counselor is usually a little uncomfortable for most people. But this time was different. To my surprise, I got nothing but good vibes from this lady and was at total peace with her. There were no red flags, no questioning her ability to trust, and no weakness was sensed on my side. In fact, I knew within the first 15 minutes she was a good match for me and I left feeling totally secure in going back to her again.

I did go back, and in fact, Mona is still my counselor today, not that I see her much any more, but I know she is there for me if I need her.

Little to my knowledge did I really understand why I was needing to see someone. All I really knew was that I was not totally happy and I struggled to find REAL peace within myself. Something was missing. Something Pat could not fulfill but I needed desperately. This bad girl side of me was coming from somewhere I never encountered before.

Other than that, life was good, and personally I think most would think I had life by the booty. The only problem is, I am NOT like most people. I will never claim to be your average person, because I am far from normal. Just ask my sister Diane. Not saying that is good or bad... just saying. So my meetings with Mona became a regular thing for a long time.... years.

Meanwhile, I started searching. What does that exactly mean?... searching? I have to be brutally honest here, *I think* (at the time) I am NOT being totally satisfied sexually. At least THAT is what *I think* it is.

It doesn't matter what we do—it's never enough for me. How do I fix this? Something is obviously wrong with this picture but why? Session after session, I finally make a decision I need to step out. Mona is very reluctant in my decision to do such a thing. But I need to find myself and get to the bottom of this swirling world pool I am living in.

Have I mentioned before that I go THROUGH the mountain and not around it?

Pat loved me, but agrees to allow me to step out, as long as I know where I lay my head at night. Part of me resented the fact that she accepted my plea to do this. This was SO NOT my REAL wish in our relationship, but something had to give somewhere, because where I was, was not working for me and I am running out of options.

Right there is a prime example of Big Helen and Little Helen not agreeing. Little Helen wants to step out, Big Helen not so much. I'm only being honest, I want you the reader to see the process in which I traveled, so maybe you won't make the same big mistakes I have.

I also want to tell you this is NEVER a good idea; you will see why as the story unfolds. Living through this experience, I will NEVER tell you this was the right route. Even today... this is the route of destruction and no return.

So I went on the search for what I thought I wanted, personal ad after personal ad. I finally found what I thought met my criteria. He was a blonde, semi-pro tennis player, but he was NOT what I was looking for and I left disappointed.

So what is it again I am even looking for? Oh, yeah, "Complete Fulfillment."

So where exactly do I find THIS? I kept searching internet ad after internet ad. Months go by, person after person.

Until... I came across this man who looks like a god, built with muscles everywhere and I mean everywhere. His name was Willie and I will tell you it was love/lust at first sight for me. I did not know what I was getting myself into with him.

I managed to let him break my heart into a whole bunch of tiny pieces. Really, I should have called him "Slick Willie" because I found out later that not only was he still legally married, his wife was home, sick, and dying of cancer.

This man totally lied to me and told me **he was NOT married.**

Believe me, I did ask him before we ever met: he even lived alone. I was sick, and I only had myself to blame for this for allowing myself to think that I can play in life this way. But it didn't stop there. There were more, and this went on for two more years.

Oh, did I tell you Pat and I broke up? Go figure... right ?

Stepping out on your partner (or throwing another person in the middle), is NEVER the answer to a problem UNLESS you want OUT of that relationship, because that is exactly what you are going to get. Subconsciously, that is exactly what I wanted but didn't know how I was going to achieve it. I was done and literally threw the relationship to the curb.

Again, **I am not a Settler... I am a Pioneer.**

I HAVE to get to the root of the problem within myself. That is how I have grown and learned to be a better me... today/tomorrow. I need to know myself better so I will stop this uncommitted behavior.

I am not saying that all these one-night stands with all these people were right because you and I both know they're NOT. It is my past, and I will tell you it was not all in vain. I learned plenty about myself—Past, Present and Future.

Some people have alcohol or drug addictions, pornography, or anger. Mine was sex. Does not make mine any more right or wrong? It just is—it's a part of me, and I need to adjust my life accordingly from now on. I must protect myself (or cover myself) daily in Jesus because the strength to succeed does NOT come from me. The moment I stop believing, that is the moment I fall. Believe me, I know because I have tried it with no avail.

I am going to write something I pray I don't regret. I have been free from this burden for almost two years. Usually when I say anything about my progress to anyone, I get double-time attacked by the horn bearing fellows. I am hoping that by writing and not saying it out loud, this does not take place because I am protected by the blood of Jesus.

We all have the means of stopping him (satan) by the power given to us through Jesus Christ once we are Christians. It's using the power given to us that seems to be the problem.

I am no angel, believe me, but I do know my place in Christ.

Ephesians 6:12
"For our struggle is not against flesh and blood but against the rulers, against the authorities the powers of this dark world and against the spiritual forces of evil in heavenly realms."

This verse is the absolute key to why I am even writing this book. If you get nothing out of this book, please understand this one verse. It WILL change the course of your life forever!!

I have learned something major–something so important it can literally change the way you live your life every day. This one verse can change the course of mankind because if you can understand where the problem is coming from, you can STOP it for good.

I am going to start another chapter because this is a whole new topic on its own.

This next chapter IS the key to this book: This battle is NOT ours to fight but God's.

30

EPHESIANS 6:13

"For our struggle is NOT against flesh and blood, but against the rulers, against the authorities the powers of this dark world and against the spiritual forces of evil in heavenly realms."

I am sitting here thinking WHAT can I entitle this chapter that will make the reader understand HOW very important this verse really is? I think this will do.

I did not understand what I was searching for. Totally confused and desperate, I continued to go through men like I was starving for affection, but it was cold and heartless.

Then one night, I got this lame brain idea to go to a... well, let's just call it a 'swingers club.' This was new to me and I had no idea WHAT I would find there. I was feeling very adventurous and anxious. I thought, *What harm can it be to just go in and look around a little bit?*

When I walked in, there was this hallway and when I walked down the hallway, I came to these two big doors. If I remember correctly, they were red in color.

I started talking to one of the service people there. He was carrying a stack of white towels. I said, "This is my first time here." He said, "Welcome, would you like to go in and look around?" I said, "Sure." I had no clue what I would find on the other end of those big red doors, but I was excited to find out.

He proceeded to open the door and said, "Go ahead and walk through." When I tell you *I was nowhere near ready to experience this, I MEAN IT!*

He pulled open the big door, and all I heard was moaning and groaning like demons. It was the most eerie sound I have ever heard in my life. I sensed evil and darkness like never before. I was now, very reluctant to walk in. I could feel the force of evil so strong that it felt like a force of wind hitting my whole body at once. I stepped one foot in front of the other, as if walking into a dream or nightmare.

My God, I thought, *what am I doing here?*

The overbearing sounds and naked bodies piled on each other, squirming like worms or snakes, slithered on the mattresses, couches and beds. They lined all the walls in that big room. There had to be 50-60 people moaning and groaning. I walked to the end, and it opened up into another room with two more piles of snakes.

The evil was so strong that all the hairs on my body were standing up and I knew when I walked out of that room that something was very wrong. I walked through the big red doors and just kept walking right out the second set, straight to my car like a zombie. I sat in my car seat and thought, *I will NEVER do that again.*

Little did I know it was too late... I was not leaving there alone.

I knew something didn't feel right, but I could not figure out *what* it was.

31

SIX TWENTY IN THE MORNING

That other person was not me.

I have this handyman named Bob who comes over and helps me by doing odd jobs around the house. He seems like a good guy, honest, hard worker, and a Christian. Well, two weeks ago I had asked him to come over to help me with a project in the house. Pat just happened to be home, and this was the second time she had met him. After he had completed the project, I took him home. When I returned, I walked in the door and Pat says, "So what do you know about Bob?" I said, "He is a very nice Christian guy, studies The Word, and does good work. Why?" She says, "I am interested in him. You think he would go to church with us tomorrow?" I said, "Really, I don't know. I can ask him." I have known him for about seven months, and I did trust him for the most part. I thought this could be a good match.

Bob did go to church with us, and Pat took him out to lunch afterwards, because it happened to be his birthday that Sunday.

All seemed fine, until I couldn't get to sleep that night until she got home from going on a date with him. Two days later, they went out on another date and that evening, I started crying (or should I say wailing) until she came home at 12:30 p.m. Mind you, I am up at 3:15 a.m. every morning so I can be at work by 5 A.m. Then these unbelievably strong feelings of anger, sadness, hate, and jealousy started festering inside of me like a freight train. I am beside myself. I do not understand where these feelings are coming from. I like Bob and I trust him, and why wouldn't I want Pat to be happy? This just looked like a real good thing. These feelings kept getting stronger and stronger, more anger, spite, and jealousy was brewing inside of me. I didn't even want her touching me or talking to me. When I thought of them two together, it made me so sick I could not eat. I lost 15 pounds in 10 days.

I was averaging 2½ to 4 hours of sleep per night and was working ten-hour days. Every day became worse with how I was treating her; I actually told her not to bring him over because I was afraid of what I might do. Choking him out seemed like a good start.

I was battling all day and most of the nights. I was obsessed with this whole situation, and every day that passed, my thoughts would get worse. The anger festered in me like a rotten piece of meat. I would pray, *Lord help me get rid of these horrible thoughts,* but they would only get worse... lots worse.

I contacted my counselor, Mona, on Thursday, and I let her know how bad I was feeling. She had me come and see her immediately. We talked it out and I remember saying, "This is so stupid, why am I feeling this way; it's just not like me. I am the one who set them up. I should be OK with this." She thinks I may be mourning over the fact that I did not think she would be able to move on. I am still confused when I leave her office, but I try to take it all in the best I can.

Friday night Pat goes to see Bob again. I am so full of deep-seated anger with just the mention of his name, I could kill.

Pat says, " I am free tomorrow night (Saturday). Why don't we watch a movie together?"

I agree until Saturday night approaches and I am trying to find Pat. I look in the bathroom, then the bedrooms. She is not in the house. I go to the back door, open it up, and I see her on the phone.

Instant rage enters my whole body—I am beside myself. I go lie down in the bedroom with the lights off and begin to shake with anger. I can hear her coming down the hallway. She opens the door and says, "What are you doing"? I say, "I think I am going to go on a motorcycle ride." She says, "OK," then leaves and shuts the door. I am fit to be tied that she is so nonchalant. I put my shoes on, grab my keys, and walk out the door. I sit on my motorcycle and realize how I want to self-destruct at this very moment and head to a bar.

Mona and I talked about this and she said, "Find a safe place to go." So I call my Harley buddy, Kat, an old roommate and friend of mine of 19 years, and ask her what she is doing? She replies, "Watching T.V. and drinking a beer." I asked if I could join her, and she said, "Sure, but bring some beer." I am almost out." I stop at the local gas station to pick up a 12-pack, and I am on my way. I pull up and the garage door opens, in goes my motorcycle. She and I both know I will not be going anywhere tonight. I got halfway through my second beer and I could already feel the buzz coming on. I started laughing and when I told her, she said, "Helen, when was the last time you ate?" I said, "About 9:00 this morning," and it is now around 8 at night.

"She says, " Well, you won't take long, are you hungry?" I refused any food offer she gave me and by my fourth beer the room started spinning. I remember her looking at me and saying, "Are you ready?" I replied, "Yes," and off to bed I went, and passed out in less that 30 seconds I am sure.

We talked about a lot of things that night, and I told her I was going to give myself two weeks to get through this. She said, "17 years is a long time. There is no way you are getting through this in two weeks."

117

My thought was *watch me.* She had asked me more than once if I was going to text Pat and let her know I was safe. My reply was, "Absolutely not." She said, "You are punishing her for something you agreed on and this is not her fault." I said, "I don't care," and at the time I really didn't

The next morning (Sunday) was a little different; I was feeling just a little guilty, but not enough to text or call Pat. Then about 7:30 a.m., I get a text from Pat. "Are you going to church today?" I am still full of anger and did not want to reply. Kat pretty much insisted again that I was punishing her for something that was not her fault. I did text her back but did not want to.

By the start of the second week I was crying so hard at work uncontrollably that I went home sick on Wednesday. I could not focus on my job. I am a punch press operator, operating presses from 60 to 200 tons of pressure coming down repeatedly. It's not a good place to be without a clear mind. Yet every day I came home so exhausted, and I still had a hard time sleeping. I am half- way into my second week of this, and my thoughts are so violent I am actually afraid of what I might do. I cannot understand why I have become so full of hate and anger toward them. This does not make sense to me, and it's not getting any better.

Mona and Pat get the same text message from me Wednesday morning at 8:57 a.m. August 1st. "The sadness—is it supposed to come and go? Had a good and mostly happy day yesterday. Today, very, very, sad again—can't seem to stop crying… may go home. Is this normal?"

Mona responds with, "Yes it's normal," and tells me to go home if I am able, and to cry it out—let myself feel the pain. I am thinking, 'I thought I already did that.'

Pat responds with, "Yes, it's normal," and tells me she will be coming home at noon. I wailed for almost an hour, allowing myself to feel the pain as told to do. It just seemed to enrage the deep- seeded evil feelings inside me. I am so confused…isn't this supposed to release or lessen the pain not intensify it? My thoughts are growing more evil in content like thoughts of suicide are entering my head as well as thoughts of murder or harm to others. Thoughts I have never had to deal with before. I mean very, very evil and dark. The sorrow is so heavy that it is becoming almost unbearable at times.

I can only remember experiencing this overbearing sadness once in my life. I was 16 and almost lost my life that night, but this is not clicking in my head. I am just focused on the obsession I am having with this evil couple trying to hurt me deeply…well, this is what I am seeing and feeling at the time. A real mix up of the facts in my life. I do not see hope or any type of release—only a deeper and deeper heartfelt sorrow as time passes.

Thursday, I texted Mona. "I believe I am done, I am shutting this mourning sh*t off. I am going to give her my wedding rings back and our wedding album and our printed vow from church and move on with my life. No more feeling sorry for myself, I have a new life ahead of me now. GOD IS GOOD! Thanks, Woman, "could not have got where I am without you!!"

I went home that night, gathered up my rings, our wedding album and printed vow and put them all in a big box. I did the dishes while I waited for her to come home from the dentist. My thought was, *I am over this, I am in control of me and I have allowed myself to mourn 11 days. I am done with it. It's been long enough.*

Besides, I just could not understand why I was making such a big deal of all this anyway. Isn't this what I wanted in the first place for her to be able to move on and be happy? All the times I was in Mona's office, I remember crying only two times and both times were because we had gotten into a discussion about Pat not being able to move on.

That really hit me hard thinking I do not want to leave her alone. She told me in the beginning of our relationship that this one was it for her. If this didn't work she would move to another country and work with the animals and would be done with people. I did not want to be the one to drive her to that point in her life and have always felt the pressure of that on me.

She walked in the door and we sat down to eat and I said, "I want to talk to you and need to give you something." She smiled at me and said, "OK" I said, "Today, August 2nd we are getting a divorce from each other." Her smile immediately left her face and part of me was very sad and another part of me had great happiness in seeing her sadness. I gave her the box and she saw the wedding album and said, "What am I supposed to do with this?"

I said, "I don't care, I don't want it. You can burn it if you want."

Then she reached into the bottom and pulled out the little black ring box and a look of real sadness came across her face and a part of me was so saddened that tears started to fall down my face and she welled up with tears herself.

Then again, a great happiness almost like a feeling of satisfaction came across me. Not understanding this, we hugged and I said, "I want to kiss you one last time and I will never kiss you again."

I thought, *What… did I just say that?* She leaned over to kiss my lips, and this uncontrollable feeling to grab her head and force a French kiss on her came over me. Without another thought I stiffened my body to control it from making any movement. This was harder than I thought. It felt like someone was pushing my head from behind as if to try and drown me in a tub of water, and I was pushing back to stop my head from moving. This was so out of character for me, it wasn't funny.

A quick thought came over me, *What in the world am I thinking, why would I even think about forcing her to do anything and ask her to kiss me…why?*

The next morning, I got up to get ready to go to work and this thought came over me, *Now that you are divorced from her, you don't owe her anything. Now it's game on. She thought I was mean before —just wait and see, this is going to be fun.*

I walk into the living room with five minutes left before I have to leave for work. I sat on the recliner, put my elbows on my knees, my head in my hands, and begin to pray. *Lord, please, I am begging you to help me stop these thoughts, please I can't take this anymore, please, please help me, I don't know what is wrong with me but this is not right, please help me in the name of Jesus.*

I get up grab my Harley keys and walk out the door; I pull out of the driveway on my motorcycle and I am still crying and such a deep, deep sorrow comes over me. I can hardly concentrate. Tears are running down my face as I pull up to the stoplight, and the pain is almost unbearable.

I am speeding up to enter onto US19 and my sorrow is consuming me. It has now overwhelmed my whole being. I arch my back up to the sky and shout at the top of my lungs. *GOD, I AM BEGGING YOU WITH EVERYTHING IN ME, PLEASE STOP THIS PAIN. I CAN'T BEAR IT ANY LONGER. IT'S TOO HEAVY, I AM BEGGING YOU, PLEASE!! IN THE NAME OF JESUS CHRIST SURROUND ME WITH YOUR ANGLES LORD, HELP ME GET THOUGH THIS PLEASE! I AM BEGGING YOU WITH EVERYTHING IN ME, WHY AREN'T YOU LISTENING TO ME GOD PLEASE HEAR ME...PLEASE!!*

I repeat this over and over. I am now approaching Brian Dairy a crossroad on 66th Street. The light is red and something in me is telling me to run the red light. I am crying out loud, fighting inside myself, I need to make a decision soon the light is still red and I am approaching fast.

I manage to let my hand off the throttle to slow my approach, then I yell out loud, "NO!" and I slam on the breaks and come to a screeching halt.

Tears are still falling as I put my feet on the ground and think, *What the hell am I doing?* as a car goes flying by.

I get to work and not even five minutes into my job, and the crying is starting up again with this incredible amount of sadness surrounding my whole being again. These evil thoughts start to come into my head. Thoughts of how to hurt Pat and Bob and take myself out of this life—all in one big bang.

The thought in my head gave me specifics on how to come into the room, what to say, where to stand, and how to hold the gun to do the most impact.

I am not going to go into detail about this but I need to let you know. I have proof that satan is alive and well and he wants nothing better than to destroy each and everyone of us.

I text Pat at 5:49 a.m.: "Please, please pray 4 me, I am not doing well." I know she is still asleep but I am pleading for my life here. I will take any help I can get from anyone at this moment. My next thought is when she is up and answers me I am going to text her to "hide the gun from me." I am trying to counteract the thoughts going through my head before something serious happens.

All this time, I am repeatedly crying out to God, and still trying to run my machine at work, not a good idea… I know. I am thinking, *if I don't stop crying soon my boss will be in, and I will have to leave and go home.* He will not allow me to run my machine in this condition; it's way too dangerous. I am trying to convince myself to stop crying, but it seems to only intensify my situation. All these prayers I am sending up, and I am not getting any kind of relief what so ever.

I stop my machine, stand up and close my eyes. It then hits me like a two by four right between my eyes. *He cannot answer my prayers if I have any type of sin in my life, I need to confess and repent.*

I look at the clock, and it is now 6:20 a.m. I bow my head, *Lord, please forgive me for all these evil thoughts and all the things going on in my head.*

At that split second, I feel this incredible release from the bottom of my feet out through the top of my head leave my body. All my prayers that moment just got answered by my God; King of Kings and Lord of Lords.

The crying stopped, all the pain is gone, I have this calmness fill my whole being, and this unbelievable peace consumes me, all in a split second of time. It hits me right then, I was demonically oppressed. I think *What…. where did that come from?* and I go on with my day as if nothing ever happened.

I got home that evening and yell at the doorway, "I am home, this time it is really me!" I hug Pat and tell her how sorry I am for everything in the last two weeks, and explain what was going on in my head. Tell her how happy I am that it's working out between her and Bob, and I mean it.

That other person was not me.

Demonic spirits are REAL and there is only one way to get rid of them or cast them out, and that is by using The Name of 'Jesus'. I had used The Name of Jesus, but He could not answer my prayer, because I had not confessed my sin. It's very important to ask God to forgive you of any sin before you start praying for anything.

He is Holy, and we must be clean before... Coming to Him.

The Third Commandment is: "Thou shall not use The Lord God's Name in vain."

This is why when people use His name in swear words… … it really is a sin.

Demons have to move with the mention of HIS HOLY name....

THAT IS JUST HOW POWERFUL IT IS.

I am certain that I picked up that demon when I entered the room at the swingers club. I truly believe it was more than one but it doesn't matter because my GOD REIGNS. They are gone and the lesson is learned. Don't play in swinger clubs, they are full of demons.

We are not equipped to fight evil on our own, and God did not intend us to do so. Without Him we will never be victorious in fighting evil. We are not super heroes, we are only human. Don't get me wrong—counselors and doctors are needed, but the REAL VICTORY comes from THE LORD.

This is MY life the one God chose for me and NO ONE else.

"God is Lord of my life, and before Him I stand righteous because of the blood His Son Jesus Christ shed for me on the cross. There is NO person alive today who can tell me that I am not doing God's will. If you think you can, I need to be the first to tell you, Beware, God is just... judge not that ye may not be judged. Who of you stands to cast that first stone? To you I say, Please be careful, be very careful, know the TRUE facts before you start throwing. I am protected by the Lord God Almighty, maker of Heaven and Earth and through Him, lives shall be saved, lives shall be changed."

I just re-read what I wrote and I'm second-guessing myself, because it is so bold. In my head, I prayed, *Is this really of you Lord? Who am I to write like this?* I have always prayed that the words in this book would not be mine, but God's. I questioned God, and said *Lord, are you sure this is what I am supposed to write?* In my head I prayed, *Please give me a sign Lord, I need to know for sure this is what you want.* I was told that my sister walking in the room would confirm it. Just as that thought ended, I heard my sister in the other room say to her friend, "I will be right back," and she turned the doorknob and opened the door and walked in. I turned my head and said to my sister, "Why did you come in here?" She said, "I don't know, something just told me to come in here."

OK I am convinced; I will leave those words there.

You see, we are all predestined; God is ALL knowing He knew the course of my life before I ever drew my first breath.

pre•des•tine |prēdestin|
verb [trans.] (usu. be predestined)
(of God) destine (someone) for a particular fate or purpose :Calvinists believed that every person was predestined by God to go to heaven or to hell.
• determine (an outcome or course of events) in advance by divine will or fate: she was certain that fate was with her and everything was predestined | [as adj.] (predestined) our predestined end.

I am NOT saying this course of being gay is what God wanted for my life because it's not. He does give us the freedom to choose good, bad, right or wrong. All I am saying is He knew my course, my journey. He knew everything was going to take place before my existence. He also allows things to happen in our lives. Because HE gives us a free will, it's out of love for HIM, I have chosen to leave that lifestyle.

This life style is no different than people living out of wedlock. That's right, living with someone you are not married to and having sexual relations with. This sin is a sin upon yourself not toward God, but it's still sin and separates us from God.

Always has, and always will.

I Cor. 10:13 (NIV)
"No temptation has seized you except what is common to man. And God is faithful; He will not let you be tempted beyond what you can bear. But when you are tempted, He will also provide a way out so that you can stand up under it."

The devil is behind ALL the bad, negative, and evil things, but we like to blame God when anything goes wrong.

I have never heard anyone blame the devil except for maybe, "The devil made me do it." But the truth is, the devil can't not make us do anything. He can tempt us, but it's our own choice, just like Adam and Eve.

My choice on being with a woman for 17 years of my existence was due to being damaged goods. But isn't that just how the devil wants us to be... damaged or broken separated from all the good God has for us?

I simply chose to NOT let those who abused me in my childhood be victorious in my life. Why? Because this is MY life!

You don't get that right to have that much power over me... ..
unless... I allow it.

I fought in the pits of (my own) hell to change my course of life.

My counselor, Mona, is right. "I should not be here, I should be a drug addict, prostitute or dead." By this world's standards.

But I am NONE of these.

By the Grace of My Heavenly Father, I stand before you A CHANGED WOMAN!

The pits of hell shall fall before me, because Christ lives in me and I am the daughter of The Most High God, and He Reigns Victorious in me!
Amen

32

MY ADDICTION

This world is nothing but a battlefield of good and evil.

I do not like to fail and admit defeat. It's just not my way. In fact it's totally gut wrenching for me, but sometimes we have to do things we don't like or want to do just to save ourselves from destruction. I am admitting that I have a problem to myself, to the one I love, and to my God.

Stop... I just wrote something, and didn't realize I wrote it... I wrote, "I do not like to fail and admit defeat..." but it is exactly the opposite. What feels like failure to me is actually strength because by NOT admitting I have a problem, I never really admit, see it, or deal with it. My pride stands in the way of ever winning over the situation because I fool myself into thinking there is no problem. I then continue to wallow in the mud hole I am lying in, until my pride decides to give it up, and for some.... that day never comes.

I wrote a poem about my addiction.

MY ADDICTION

How do I stop this, merry-go-round Lord?
How do I get off, this hellish ride?
No more happiness, in my heart Lord,
When I'm consumed, with wrongful pride.
How do you love me, Lord I ask thee?
How do you forgive me for what I do?
"For it's by grace my precious child,
I hung on that cross for you".
I took my eyes off of you Lord,
With satan knowing what to do.
I broke my covenant, and my promise,
To the one I gave it to.
How do you love me, Lord I ask thee?
How do you forgive me for what I do?
"For it's by grace my child I tell you".
I hung on that cross for you".
Now I stand here broken hearted,

Knowing I can't take it all back.
Lord protect me, Lord please help me,
To stay on the right track.
How do you love me, Lord I ask thee?
How do you forgive me for what I do?
"For it's by grace my child I tell you".
I hung on that cross for you".
How do I, forgive myself Lord,
How do I, let it all go?
Or do I learn, from my mistakes Lord,
And learn to reap, what I sow.
How do you love me, Lord I ask thee?
How do you forgive me for what I do?
"For it's by grace my child I tell you,
I gave up my ALL, for you".

-Helen On Wheelz 3/14/2010

Sometimes satan (I refuse to capitalize his name, unless it's the first word of a sentence), uses our own mistakes to keep us trapped. It never surprises me how low satan will go to try an keep us down. He loves shame and he loves pride because it keeps us from growing. Satan owns those two words and they are NOT of God.

This world is really nothing but a battlefield of good and evil and we are the playing pieces. No matter how you look at it, satan will always be there to help you self-destruct. He has that way of making it look so appealing. Have you ever heard of *a wolf in sheep's clothing?* Well, that is how satan really is: he wants you to think he is all warm and cuddly. Like he has our backs, but in reality he is looking for someone, anyone, to devour. He'll be the first to tell you, "Oh it's not so bad." He'll say, "Hey, you will be cool if you do that." "Nobody will ever know if you take only one." "Besides, it feels good. Don't you want to feel good?"

He is that little voice that cries in our heads. The problem is, just because we like it, doesn't mean it's right or good for us. There are always consequences to every decision we make. I am no stranger to any of this and as sure as I am writing this book, none of you are either. The problem is that the consequences always become part of our lives somewhere down the road. If you don't feel them now, there is a good possibility you may in the future.

Here's an example of a very bad decision I made in my past that is still affecting me to this day as I am writing, at age 44. I started smoking cigarettes when I was seven years old. I used to smoke on the farm in the summer (not every summer), but probably two or three of them. I used to smoke occasionally in my 20's and 30's. I was one of those who could smoke one or two and not touch another cigarette for months. I have bought maybe five packs my whole life and never finished a single pack, always ending up throwing or giving most of them away. If I ever felt like I was getting hooked, I would stop smoking cold turkey. I don't like things to control me, and after years of just occasionally smoking, I started getting this deep cough that actually drained me of my energy. I went to the doctor and she asked me if I smoked. I said, "No, not really maybe five or six cigarettes a year, very rarely on occasion." She said, "You have bronchitis and you need to stop immediately."

I said, "What? How can that be? I hardly even smoke." She asked me, "So, how old where you when you started?" "Wow," I thought... "let's see. I was pretty young. It started back on the farm; probably smoked most summers between seven and eleven." She said, "Are you serious? That is why, your lungs were not fully developed—you started smoking before puberty."

Can you believe something I did over 40+ years ago is still affecting me today? That is what I call consequences from a very bad decision. We all have to live with those in our lives. In my mind I think, *OK, I messed up. I will stop smoking for good because I do not want it to get any worse.* It's fair and understandable, and I will adjust my life to protect myself from any further health problems.

The consequences that are really tough to swallow or understand are the ones that come from other people's wrong doings or the ones that stem from our childhood. Those are really not fair to me, but I know they are there. Those are the ones I am writing about right now in this chapter. Actually it's one of those that I am trying to get through in my own life right now, in my 40's. It's causing me to crawl into the gutters to find myself so I can learn to stay out of it or just plain deal with it in the safest way possible for me. This is not about my family, my job, my friends, or anything else that affects my life. This is about teaching and showing Little Helen that *what she thinks she is looking for, is not and will not, REALLY satisfy her in the end.*

How do I teach her that, you may be asking? Simple, I allowed her to walk into it. To feel it, touch it, smell it, taste it and whatever it involves. Remember I (Big Helen), get to pick and choose the safest path. Also, don't forget the golden rule. She must ALWAYS, ALWAYS learn something from it. I walked her as deep as we had to go without staying there.

Example: say it's drugs she is thinking, she's wanting. I (big Helen) would ask myself questions like. "Why are you feeling the need to try or do this particular product?" The answer may be, 'because other friends are, or 'it makes me happy.'

In the past, I did allow her to smoke pot, but here is what she has learned from that experience. There are pros and cons just like anything else in life.

The Pros: (+)
(+) It makes me laugh uncontrollably/happy
(+) I loved the feeling I got
(+/-) I felt a very relaxing and calming effect over my whole body, like the whole world could blow up and I just didn't care, everything was going to be fine.

The Cons: (-)

(-) I felt very unsafe if I smoked before entering a public place (paranoid).

(-) It burns my throat

(-) It cost a lot for just a little

(-) I didn't like the fact that it's illegal

(-) It truly affected my memory to the point when I was driving down a street, I didn't know where I was and I was on a street I had driven often. That was a bit scary to say the least.

So, what Little Helen learned from that experience is it simply is not worth it. The Cons out weighed the Pros.

After that experience, I really had no desire to try other forms of substances besides drinking, and even with that, through my journeys, I know my limits. In the chapter, "My trip to Maryland," I talk about one of my drinking experiences. I have never just sat in a mud hole and stayed there. I have always learned and moved on. That is how I have gotten as far as I have. It doesn't take rocket science, because believe me, I am no Einstein here. I just make myself learn something from every step I take, that's all… it's not that hard.

This is about taking care of the inner child who (thinks she) is in need of something I (big Helen) never knew existed, but as I go through life, I am continually learning lessons.

Now that I found a problem, I need to find the safest way possible to give her what she (thinks she) needs with out disrupting my life too drastically. Without harming me and finding a safe place to get what she (thinks she) needs to be happy. At this point, I am hoping I will find the peace inside I am looking for, and at some point she will be fulfilled enough and won't feel she needs it anymore. I am willing to give her things that are not harmful to her, that are not self destructive, and are taken in moderation with definite boundaries in place. Again, like a parent teaches a child, I must grow her up to learn the good and bad as well as the right and wrongs.

However long it takes for her to understand, is how long this must be. The only thing I ask from her is growth through whatever I allow her to go through. She must learn something from everything she has endured, and begin to change into a better and stronger person.

I am the one who is controlling her through this process. She does NOT control me although she used to.

That is the key to this whole learning stage that I am allowing her to go through. It's about helping her grow up and learn.

That is my mission as the adult, and sometimes these things aren't very pretty, but it is the reality of this sickness. It is also how I have gotten her to become a better and stronger person throughout the years. This although, is the hardest thing I have ever had to help Little Helen go through. I believe it must be done in order to make her well for our future. These are the immaturities I have because of what was done to me as a little child, or the consequences of the sinful acts that were forced upon me.

Now, I could just sit and feel sorry for myself and lead myself down a self–destructing, self-mutilating path by wallowing in my self-pity, and let life pass me by while I learn nothing. Just keep doing the same thing over and over, year after year.

I could get on drugs and never get off.... many do. I could become a prostitute, find a pimp who treats me like I feel or think I should be treated.

Speaking of that:
I watched a show on prostitution and some of the ladies were saying they really believe their pimp cares for them. I guess, I can understand to some point why they may feel that way because the pimps give them what they NEED to exist. Basics, like food and shelter. And... maybe they have a pimp who is actually not beating them,
but how is that REALLY love?

If I grew up in a manure pile, do I think I stink?

Do I think everyone around me stinks?

Or... am I content with the stench, because we all smell the same?
For me, I saw and could smell the stench because I looked up.
But I was in that manure pile, myself.

I saw something better—something beautiful, and I wanted that with all my heart.

To be totally honest, I wanted anything to stop this pain...yes, but I was also willing to seek REAL happiness with everything in me.... no matter the cost. For me that was following someone I knew who had the happiness that I wanted so badly...for me that was my high school teacher, Sherry.

So my choice is to stand tall and not allow my wrongdoers of my past to control my future, and strive to become the best I can be.

Teaching others to do the same, is even a bigger kick in the face to the people of my past as well as satan.

This is not a journey to walk alone. I have had many people help me alone the way.

I am doing this with the help of counselors but most of all, My God (The Glass Blower), whom I trust as my true anchor. I know my counselor does not like this process I feel I really need to get through, but I know I will prove to her in the end that this is really the only way for me to get to the other side. It is also the reason I have grown as fast as I have. When I see a problem, I must find a way to fix it, by allowing Little Helen to experience some things to help her, so she can learn from them.

Take smoking pot for instance; a lot of us have tried it, but most of us outgrew it. So there is no problem. The problem only sets in when you never grow to move on.

A big red flag should be going off in your head right now!

The question you should be asking yourself is, "Why am I not moving on from this and growing?" Think about it!!

Without growth... comes what? DEATH! Without growth your addition becomes a crutch and completely enables you.

I found a couple quotes in the paper from a coach at UCLA who passed away. I thought they were very fitting.

"Failure is not fatal, but failure to change might be." Another one, "If you're not making mistakes, then you're not doing anything. I'm positive that a doer makes mistakes." – John Wooden 1910-2010
(Voltaire)

Today's date is 1/8/16 and it has been well over four years since I actually have written more than a poem or two. It has taken me that long to finally go through this last major journey in my life. I can finally say I have learned all I needed to lean to move on with my life and I am not willing to go back into it ever again. I have peace within myself, like never before.

I am also ready to tell you what this addiction is, which I did not feel I would ever disclose. Since it no longer has power over me, IN JESUS NAME, I am taking the power away by admitting it to you as well as myself. Admitting an addiction is half the battle to contouring it. I have stopped fighting myself and have given it to God.

I have a sexual addiction, which is not surprising considering the childhood I lived through. When you are exposed to such drastic situations as a child, it's almost natural that there are drastic consequences.

I just thank God that this addiction showed it's ugly head in my 40's when I was older and responsible to control and protect myself from things that I may not have in my youth. I am not going to go into all the brutal details, although many of them are mentioned in this book. All I am going to say is, "I have been around the block more than a few times, in different vehicles."

I was ending a 17-year homosexual relationship at the time. I was totally faithful for over 15 years of that relationship, so to me this was very drastic and very out of the ordinary.

I am now in my 50's writing this. I was in my upper 40's when going through this and a lot of thought went into each situation, unlike my 20's when I was flying by the seat of my pants and carefree.

I held a full-time job, owned a home, car, worked out regularly, and held onto what was a very real relationship to me. What I allowed myself to get tangled up in, was way more than I ever wanted in the first place. Do I regret any of them? Part of me regrets all of them and another part of me regrets none of them.

Because, I learned something from each and every one of them about myself: some things good, but most of the time it was just bad and ugly things.

Remember, Little Helen is alive and well and is looking for that old familiar feeling of when she was being violated repeatedly. This is the sick part of it all— the consequences I was talking about. That's a part of this whole dysfunction that is not easy by any means for me to talk about much less write about, but we all have our own way of getting through life… this was mine.

How did I get through it?

I looked this ugly dysfunction right in the face, eyeball to eyeball. I learned why that sick feeling felt good to Little Helen. I allowed her to go back with each person for one reason or another. Then when I had enough, where I learned about myself, I shut it down cold turkey. (I by no means am saying anyone should even do as I did but this is my story and the truth).

Example of something I learned about myself, hang on.... this is a big one... Why did I like to feel pain while having sex?... This is a big one for a lot of woman who have ever been abused. Pain! Yes, PAIN something I was so very familiar with. Believe it or not, but to some of us, this is a very comforting feeling. This again is part of the sickness.

IF this is NOT something you have experienced you may not want to finish reading this chapter because you will not understand the contents.

If you simply cannot resist... I CAUTION YOU! ENTER AT YOUR OWN RISK!

The question again to myself is: Why do/did I like to feel pain during sex?

For me the answer was a few different things. LET'S BE REAL! I felt I deserved it. Let me explain: I was about 5 years old when I started getting molested. (Wow, that was really hard to write, but it is the truth.) Deep down inside there was shame and guilt even though I, as an adult, know it was not my fault. That shame and guilt is what my five-year old, little Helen is carrying around, even though she was too young to stop the acts from happening. She was trapped inside me always thinking belittling thoughts.

In a little child's mind, what should happen to me if I am being naughty or bad? That's easy, I need to get punished... right? With punishment comes what...?

Pain! Yes, pain! Spankings, hard spankings or what ever else you can think of to make me feel pain because that is the key to me being punished. This is something, that is very comforting to people who have been abused sexually, mentally or physically.

We were raised thinking that we deserve to be treated that way (abusively). It became the norm for us. But it is NOT "norm" – not by any means... is it NORMAL. We who have been abused, carry around in us the "wounded/lost child of our past."

The good side of all this is... we also are WARRIORS/SURVIVORS, and I do not say that lightly. We can take more pain, disappointment, and abuse than your average human sucking air, and with God added into our lives...

We become INCREDIBLE WARRIORS in this World.

In other words, we become UNTOUCHABLE, meaning NO ONE can REALLY hurt us again.

When I say, "hurt us," I mean to the point of devastation/death.

Read the verses from the song by Tina Turner called *We Don't Need Another Hero:*
"I walk the ruins"
"Living under the Fear"
"Something Better"
"Something we can rely on"
"Life Beyond"
"The Ones they left behind"
"Got to be something Better"
"Love and Compassion"
"What do we do with our lives?"

This is a very, very powerful song with lyrics that identify with children who have suffered severely!

This is US! We were NOT meant to walk this journey called LIFE alone. People in our lives have FAILED us drastically and for most of us brutally and repeatedly. I don't know about you, but I got to the place where I just could not take another disappointment. PERIOD!

I wanted death over any more pain! My pain became THAT unbearable.

Are you feeling me?
But I looked up, and you can, too.... there is BETTER.
There is PEACE and TRANQUILITY
like you have NEVER imagined.
There is REAL Love and Compassion
if you have not found it yet... Follow me.
I can take you there.

Workbook

PART I

Making yourself well... are you ready?

I do not know where you stand with knowing a supreme being. Yes, I am talking about God. I am talking about NONE OTHER than THE FATHER of JESUS CHRIST. The book being The Holy Bible with NO religions attached, just The Holy Bible. This has been my real anchor in my journey of changing my thoughts and actions.

I guess I just got tired of people hurting me over and over again.

It seemed as though every single male in my past had betrayed me or hurt me in some way or another. I hit my breaking point and at age sixteen, was on the verge of taking my own life. You may have already read the story called 'Sweet Sixteen.'

It is going to take YOU going back into your past and facing your (what I call) demons. Meaning... all your pain, sorrow, fear, regrets, shame, anger, disappointments and there may be even more, depending on your past.

Before you actually read the next chapter "Going Back," I suggest you do each one of these things.

1. Prepare for making yourself well: *are you ready?*

2. Find a good counselor—Read Chapter "Finding A Good Counselor." This may take weeks or months.

My suggestion: take it to God in prayer.
Heavenly Father, please forgive me for all my sins. Help me to get well and find a good counselor to guide me through my journey. Lord, open my eyes to your will in my life, and teach me your ways. Please surround me with positive and godly people, and help me to become the warrior I was meant to be. In Jesus Name, Amen

3. Buy a new notebook—(for journaling)

4. Dig into 'Going Back.'

Going Back

Use the crutch but don't let the crutch use you.

I am not going to waste your time here, let's dig in.
- Pain
- Sorrow
- Fear
- Regret
- Shame
- Anger
- Abandonment
- Disappointments

Take a moment to think about each word.
Say it out loud and take yourself back to each one.
For example: say the word PAIN out loud, and think about times in your life you have felt pain. I am not talking just physical (unless it was abuse), but mental and emotional pain.

Let yourself go back to those moments in time.

Write each word on top of a page, and let yourself go back.

Do one at a time, and at your own pace. Do not rush through this.
This may take days, weeks or months. That's OK It's your journey; go at your own pace.

Take your time and really think about each word, and where in your life's journey you remember each word.

Briefly write down anything that pertains to that word and list the times you felt each one.

This may make you feel very exhausted, tired or drained of energy.

That is a sign that you are going in the right direction. I usually felt very exhausted and tired when I revisit the past.

You may feel angry, sad or actually cry.
This is ok. "Let it out." I cannot say that enough..."Let it ALL out"
Remember, you are dealing with your past and it is not easy for anyone to look back at unpleasant memories.. You are taking the road less traveled, because with it comes pain, that is why so many try to cover it up with their addictions. Once this is all over, the peace and healing will come... believe me—addressing it head on is worth every tear.

Your mood may change.
If you are being true to yourself, your mood has to change; this is part of the

134

process, I went through. I always put myself in a room by myself with no distractions, a place that felt safe to me.

These are all a part of releasing (what I call) the poisons or facing your demons. This is part of the healing process.

Take each word one at a time, at your own pace. There is no race here, so if you can only do one a day, one a month or one every six months.

It's ok... this is in YOUR time and no one else's.

You are dealing with your past and letting it go.
The letting go comes when you forgive.
I will be honest with you—the average person can NOT forgive without God, if the pain is too severe.
You must learn to "Let God in."
That's right... Let God in.
You're wondering, How do I do that, right?

Well, let me be the first to tell you it is possible... but you can't do it alone.

He (God) is the ONLY One you can TRULY rely on, who won't let you down. People will always be people, we are human, and it is in our makeup to fail.

As the song says, "Something We Can Rely On." Well... THAT IS GOD, JESUS CHRIST AND THE HOLY SPIRIT. They have not failed me yet, and my past no longer haunts me.

Do you want that freedom?
It is yours for the taking, but you must learn to forgive completely.

33

WHY I WANTED PAIN DURING SEX

It felt familiar...

Let me get back to my point, "Why I wanted pain during sex."
It goes back to my past.... I felt I deserved it, plain and simple.
I dabbled in Dom/Sub relationships, just a bit. I did not have to get too deep into it before Little Helen realized that she deserved better.... **much better!**

1. It made Little Helen feel powerless.

As a child, I was totally powerless. The people who sexually abused me were all male and were much older than I by some 8 or 30 years. I could not stop what was happening to me by brute strength. I was just too small—I was totally powerless. It was a very frustrating feeling, so now as an adult, the ONLY one I want controlling me is God... but only because I trust Him 100%. My "Little Helen" was a child when this happened to her, and the memory feels very familiar to her.

Do you understand that we only know what we are taught? This is the exact reason my first counselor told me I was **sick**. She meant **sick in the head** because Little Helen only knows what she was taught.

2. It felt familiar... the pain.

Both of these, the feeling powerless and feeling pain go in the same category. They were what I experienced before and were familiar to me in fact I can keep going and add #3, #4 and #5.

3. Little Helen felt she deserved to feel belittled.

4. The fear factor, adrenaline rush.

5. Little Helen wanted to feel used. (This is a tough one to admit.).

ALL of these, in a sick kind of way, were comforting to Little Helen. It cured her, but also taught me WHY my Little Helen was seeking these things.

Did you ever wonder why so many women have read the book: 50 Shades of Gray? Over 50 million copies have been sold worldwide.

Wonder no more! There are a lot of people out there who are involved in this lifestyle. My hope and prayer is that this book can help you understand yourself a little bit better.

Also, I hope it will help you break free from bondages and leads you to becoming the person you were meant to be.

These are all part of the sickness I was taught as a little child, when repeatedly abused Mentally, Physically and Sexually… the ugly truth. I told you I was going to be real with you, and I have to be, in order to help you understand.

I did NOT allow Little Helen to try or experience everything, because some things were just too far from moral or healthy. Through this process, I the adult got to pick and choose some things, being fully aware of what her/I was getting into. In other words, I was going into it level headed, with my eyes wide open, which is a far cry from just stumbling through bad decisions and not knowing what end is up, or knowing why I am doing something and never coming out of it.

DON'T BE THAT PERSON!

Try to learn from your mistakes… ALWAYS!

I thought through what I was going to do to help her grow stronger, or I wouldn't be allowing it at all. Again, I cannot say enough about how having someone you can trust like a counselor to help think things through and help you through the thought process, and the outcome. You really need someone to help be your sounding board and guide. It's like climbing a mountain and having that secured safety line there if you should need it.

Now don't get me wrong, I did not tell my counselor EVERY thing that was going on in my little head. Some things need not be verbalized. Remember, she had never gone though what I had and she would not be able to understand some of my thoughts. Be real with yourself, and honest and open with your counselor. I just kept in mind that, if it felt weird saying it… I didn't.

I am truly blessed to have found my counselor Mona. She has allowed me to grow within my own boundaries and not hers. This is very important because the boundaries she has set for herself would be no good for someone like me. She has never gone through in her past what I have. What happened to me was very dramatic and very unlike hers. Each one of us needs to set our own boundaries of what is good, bad, right or wrong according to our own lives. None of us needs to judge another on their journey in life.

That is God's job.

None of us is worthy of that duty in this life, simply because NONE of us is without wrong doing.

These crutches I am talking about that you are going through now, the only difference is, I didn't stay in them... I moved on, and you should too.

Use the crutch but don't let the crutch use you... get it?

Whatever crutch you are using now in your life, THAT is where you start. Example: if you are an alcoholic, drug user, addicted to pornography whatever.

A simple rule I try to live by is, "Judge not, that you may not be judged."

Each one of us has our own book to write in life and no one can write it for us.

It must be done according to the footprints we learn from, as well as the ones we leave behind.

34

PEDOPHILIA

This is by far one of the most selfish acts.

pedophilia | pedəfilēə |
noun
sexual feelings directed toward children..

Considering I was a victim of pedophilia in my childhood for a time period that seems like an eternity, I think I have a right to talk about it. Sexual abuse is such a betrayal to the core essence of a person's being. As innocent children, we trust that adults will not lead us to harm or betrayal. When this trust is broken, there are no words to express the damage it does to one's core being. To be used in such a selfish sense is horrific to a child who does not understand anything of it. It's an evil, self-centered gratification that comes from the pits of hell. There is nothing in these acts that benefits a child in any way. It steals away a child's innocence. Once the damage is done, the child is left in a mental state of mass confusion and lack of understanding. It's devastation to the body and mind of an innocent being to be exposed to this self-seeking sickness. The child carries this in the back of his or her mind for the eternity of their life on this earth. They will self-mutilate with addictions and will find endless ways to torment themselves. The devil will try to keep them feeling down and depressed as long as he possibly can—even to their death. Satan will torment and try to hold the innocent, molested children accountable for the rest of our lives, even though they had zero accountability for the things that happened to them. This is by far one of the most selfish acts mankind has on it's own kind. It is devastation, and lacks any sense of real love. It's 100% self-gratification in the most selfish way.

The only way to cope with the horrible experience of sexual abuse is through a higher being—and that being is Jesus Christ.

35

LOOKING BACK

I happened to be his victim.

I am going to ask a question:
"Do you think mankind is born being sexually attracted to little children?"

Ponder on that for a few...

"Is it innate in us to grow up to become adults with a desire to be sexual with babies or little children?"

I hope to God that you answer that question with a big fat, "NO!" Because that is the right answer.

We are on the same page so far.

Then tell me where is this coming from: Men, or mankind who are child molesters or pedophiles—(I should not just say men because there are some women out there, too)—where is this sexual desire coming from and why?

OK NOW we are getting into the meat and taters of things.

Let me go back and use myself as the example: My earliest memory of being molested was around four or five- years old, by my sister's live-in boyfriend. I remember this time frame because my bedroom was in (what is now) the spare room upstairs.

I believe her boy friend had a sexual addiction because he had hundreds, and I mean hundreds, of dirty magazines hiding in the garage rafters. I found them while playing up there with a friend from school.

He had a sexual attraction to children. I know that for a fact, because I happened to be his victim.

This is the first time I have EVER referred to myself as someone's victim, but I am strong enough today to be OK with this. He doesn't scare me, nor can he hurt me any more because I'm an adult—not a five-year old little girl.

I can't help but think, *WHAT A YELLOW-BELLIED COWARD.* REALLY. A FIVE YEAR-OLD LITTLE GIRL, AND YOU CALL YOURSELF A MAN?" Sorry!

So where does this come from... This being attracted to children? I do believe that ALL addictions are of the devil, because I KNOW they are NOT of God.

Here is proof:

2 Corinthians 3:17
"Now The Lord is The Spirit, and where The Spirit of The Lord is, there is freedom."

Being addicted to ANYTHING is not how God wants us to live.
Bondage is of the devil. He likes us under his thumb, stuck in a pit of self-mutilation and harm to the physical body and mind.

I can picture satan, rubbing his hands together and salivating over how he has fooled mankind to think we are anything other than what God designed us to be.

So we know they (addictions) are not of God.

So now lets talk about spirits.
Spirits can be good or bad.
They can be of God, and those are called angels.
They can be of the devil and those are called demons.
So we have a positive force and a negative force, battling for the top.

If you need proof The Bible tells of the fall of Lucifer.

Isaiah 14:12
How art thou fallen from heaven, O Lucifer son of the morning!

Revelation 12:9
The great dragon was hurled down – that ancient serpent called the devil, or satan, who leads the whole world astray. He was hurled to the earth and his angels (demons) with him.

So addictions, crutches, things of self -mutilation/harmful to ones self or others are NOT of God.

Let's list some Addictive Behaviors:

• Drugs
• Cigarettes
• Drunkenness
• Obesity
• Porn (of any kind)

- Dom/Sub Behavior (Extreme)
- Pedophilia
- Excessive Gambling
- Homosexuality
- Transgender
- Fits of Rage
- Hoarding (Excessive)
- Bestiality
- Abortion
- Eating of Human Waste
- Self-Mutilations (cutting, excessive tattoos and piercing)
- Incest

I could go on and on here.

These are just a few off the top of my head. These are evil spirits or what the Bible calls strongholds.

Many of these can also be taught, but I also believe they stem from the pits of hell and are meant for destruction to mankind, mentally, spiritually, and physically.

So my thought is, these spirits can be cast out of people in The Name Of Jesus. How do I know this? I have done it myself, read the Chapter entitled "Melissa." This casting out of demonic spirits is a real thing, so there can be freedom, if one wants it bad enough.

Now back to where this Spirit comes from.

I am quoting this from the book:
"THE HANDBOOK FOR SPIRITUAL WARFARE"
By Dr. Ed Murphy

Page. 122
Pornography, like prostitution, is not a victimless crime, as is often affirmed. It's victims are everywhere. It stimulates the imagination to commit mental adultery. It produces desires, contrary to God's will in our lives. It stirs the passion and sexual arousal, especially of men, which makes them temporarily potentially dangerous to women and to children.

While some 'experts' deny this, the average man knows it is true. Many men, including Christians, have (themselves) been sexually stimulated by pornography and have then been tempted to seek sex, even with unwilling women or children. How much incest and rape is due to sexual arousal stimulated by pornography!

Page. 470-471
ENTRANCE OF DEMONS INTO BROKEN PLACES
Many cases of demonization are tractable in times of trauma, particularly involving assault by another person, either sexual or physical. That a person should become demon-

ized on top of a trauma seems unfair, but who says we live in a fair world? Satan is the ruler of this world. Any world over which he rules will be an unfair world.

Demons are attracted to pain 1) they like the 'pain' and suffering; 2) pain produces powerlessness which makes their offers attractive.

Wilder notes: *When Jesus had fasted, he was hungry, and guess who showed up?*

*The attitude of Wilder and Friesen differs from the common one held by Christian counselors, psychologists, and psychiatrists who often affirm they have rarely or never discovered demons in the lives of severely abused patients. Fortunately for the victims, that attitude is beginning to change in the U.S. As I am examining the many counseling sessions I have had with Christians since I was first forced by the Lord into this ministry In the mid-1970's, **I have concluded that in the U.S., at least, sexual abuse after occult involvement is the number one cause of demonization in the life of Christians.***

I'm going to bring up another verse I have put in this book before but I believe it fits perfectly here:

Ephesians 6:12
"For we wrestle not against flesh and blood, but against principalities, against rulers of the darkness of this world, against spiritual wickedness in high places."

Matthew 5:27-28
"You have heard that it was said, 'do not commit adultery.' But I tell you that anyone who looks at a woman lustfully has already committed with her in his heart.'

So, am I fair in saying that pornography/mental adultery is a sin? That partaking in it could cause a man to rape women and children? It leads to addiction just like drugs and alcohol?

The difference I see, is drugs and alcohol are self-mutilations where pornography, if not stopped, will most likely involve others—most times innocent others.

These are called STRONGHOLDS, and they are REAL!!

What I do know about demonic spirits is they can transfer from one person to another through close contact like sex or even a hug. Actually, it can happen anytime two aura's (our energy fields) connect or touch one another.

I also believe that is how I received the evil spirits that had been oppressing me for a majority of my life—through the close contact from being sexually molested for countless years of my childhood. I would even bet my bottom dollar that a majority of the people who suffer from homosexuality and transgender issues, have also been sexually abused or traumatized in their past at some point.

If a woman is oppressed/possessed with a demon, I believe it can also pass on to her unborn child.

The devil is very cunning and will try to destroy us ANY way he can think of, fair or unfair. He feels absolutely NO sympathy and hates every one of us to the very core of his being.

How do I know this?
Good Question: I have dealt with him… read the Chapter entitled: *Six Twenty in the Morning.*

So be careful who you put yourself in close contact with—protect yourself at all costs.

I am not saying, "Don't hug people," by any means. What I am saying is, "Be aware of WHO you are coming close to physically."

This is why Christians perform what is called *laying of hands* on those oppressed with demonic spirits or strongholds. It's Aura touching Aura or Holy Spirit (living in us) touching unholy spirit.

Guess what happens to the unholy spirit? It's driven out.

The Holy Spirit is alive in us. Through The Holy Spirit and by using the Name of Jesus Christ, demons can and are being driven out of people.

Another good idea is to put your armor on BEFORE you surround yourself with a lot of people you don't know.

It's a continuation of the verse above:

Ephesians 6:13-18
"Therefore but on the full Armor of God, so that when the day of evil comes, you may be able to stand your ground, and after you have done everything, to stand. Stand firm then, with the belt of truth buckled around your waist, with the Breast Plate of Righteousness in place, and with your feet fitted with the readiness that comes from The Gospel Of Peace."

"In addition to all this, take up the shield of faith, with which you can extinguish all the flaming arrows of the evil one. Take the helmet of Salvation and The Word of The Spirit, which is The Word of God. And pray in The Spirit on all occasions with all kinds of prayers and requests. With this in mind, be alert and always keep on praying, for all the saints".

36

ABANDONMENT

A major part in my life.

Abandonment is a word I know quite well; let me count the ways. In a matter of only five minutes, I have thought of 16 different times I feel I have been abandoned in my life (so far). It all started at age two and a half. I am going to try to make these examples as short as possible. I just want you to get an idea of what happened to me at an early age and how the desperation of abandonment has played a major part in my life. Some examples are repeats from other parts of this book, while others are new descriptions.

MOM DIES

My mother died when I was two years old, which left me to be raised by my oldest sister. She had her hands full, because she had my three other brothers to raise and a son of her own. I was the youngest of eight living children. I don't know if I really was ever that close to my mom. She worked a lot, and I can't say I remember anything about her. I do know that I did feel a great sense of loss that I just couldn't identify.

The worst thing is that I remember myself feeling that her death was my fault. I felt awful about this for many years as a young girl. That's a ridiculously heavy burden to bear—let alone the shameful feelings that go with it. I even thought that maybe God took her from me because I had done something wrong. My little mind thought that maybe I didn't really deserve a mom. I cried myself to sleep many a night with that one. Little children tend to personalize things because they really don't know any better. Maybe kids are also a little self-centered because they only know of their own needs, being so young. The blame is easy to put on them—I know I did—because I believed that adults are never wrong. I thought that little kids are more likely to be wrong than the adults. As a kid, this made perfect sense!

CRYING IN CRIB

I was very young, and I remember I was in a crib crying and crying very hard. I was wearing a red one—piece pajama suit. You know, the fuzzy one with the feet attached. I was very hot and my hair was wet with sweat. I was screaming as loud as I could scream. I could hear my family say in unison, "Cry a little louder, we can't hear you!" which infuriated me to no end and made me scream until I coughed out loud and my throat hurt, as if raw. Over and over, I could hear them say this as they laughed at me because I would scream even louder. I remember standing on my bed and shaking my crib bars, as I jumped up and down in anger. My face was wet and hot and my body on fire with sweat. My whole body itched while the pajamas stuck to my skin. My face was on fire as tears ran down, soaking my pajamas even more. I was so thirsty, and no one would come—no one. I just wanted to be held, and told it was going to be OK Did no one care enough to hold me and calm me down? Am I alone in this world? What did I do to deserve this type of unloving family to feel so abandoned at such a young age?

I don't hold grudges, but I must admit that it made quite an impression in my little mind to remember that far back in a crib. I was quickly figuring out the reality of my future. I would walk this life alone.

WHERE IS DAD?

I never remember seeing my real father from the time I was eight to the age of 18. I would often wonder, "Where could he be? Does he even know where I am? Does he even care? What kind of man can just walk away from his own flesh and blood?"

I have never received a single card from him that I know of. After all those years of silence of not hearing from him, I found out that my oldest sibling was the one who was actually keeping us from him. My father passed away only seven years after I turned 18, so my time with him was very limited.

Again, I do not hold grudges. I rest peacefully in knowing my God is a just God and I will leave the feelings of my father's absence for Him.

ON A JET PLANE

The only "mother" I had after the age of two and a half, was my oldest sibling. I have a very vivid memory of being at an airport and pounding on the glass window when I was about this age (two and a half years). I was screaming, "Mom, Mom," over and over again. My sister was boarding an airplane to go to Mexico. I was crying very hard with a sick sense of desperation and panic. At the time I did not know why she was leaving me but inside my heart, I felt I would never see her again. Understand—this is the second mom I felt was leaving me for good... ...all alone. Again. The pain was very real—totally overwhelming. It felt like my beating heart was ripped out of me!

I found out later at age 18 from my step-father what had actually happened that day at the airport. I told him all I could remember was pounding on an airport window, crying of a broken heart. His eyes lit up and said, "I can not believe you actually remember that day! You were so young!" I said, "It was devastating to me, how could I not remember it?"

ON MY OWN

I remember the day that I went to some of my closest relatives to tell them that the neighbor boy had sexually violated me. The two close relatives I told were of zero help to me. Worse than being no help, they followed suit and started doing exactly the same things that the neighbor boy had done. They also sexually abused me, and it was beyond horrible. Talk about a lonely and unprotected feeling. This was the epitome of being lonely, unsafe, and unable to trust anyone—including my own flesh and blood. It was me against the world. And I knew it. It was unthinkable, and I felt that I could never really trust ANYONE ever again.

Do you wonder why I turned to God? He was the One who would always be there for me. He was the one I could trust. He would never turn His back on me.

Because of God's love, NO ONE can ever hurt me again. I trust God 100%, but really don't trust anyone else in the same way I do Him. If you can ever learn this one…you will have life by the butt. I learned that God is the One who will always love me and look after me—no matter what. Don't get me wrong—I still love and hold some of my family and close friend close to my heart, but no human can again hurt me to the point of breaking my will… NO ONE! ONLY MY GOD HOLDS THAT POSITION… PERIOD.

LEFT FOR WOLF

My oldest sibling who raised me, took up the game of bowling… that's right BOWLING. Every Wednesday when she bowled, she left her child-molesting, porn reading, Vietnam Veteran boyfriend to babysit us kids alone. I remember crying intensely—begging her not to go. But, out the door she went—every Wednesday on schedule. I think by the title of this section, you can figure out what happened to me on bowling nights. I was totally overwhelmed and helpless…. And I have never forgotten. Only by the Grace of My Holy God do I stand before you.

MY BIRTHDAY PARTY

My grade school birthday party was a total disappointment. I invited five or six friends and only one came. This has been the real reason behind why I didn't tell people my birth date for over 20 years.

I MISSED 6TH GRADE

My sibling had this wonderful idea from our neighbors to change us from the public school to a private school. The only problem was that our records never came with us. Because of this, they tested Dudie and me to see our grade levels and progress. Dudie passed with flying colors, but I failed miserably. Little did I know—I had a reading problem called dyslexia. A lot is known about it today, but little was known about dyslexia in those days. All I knew was that school was always a struggle for me. I was put back in the same class as Dudie for two years, and when I was to graduate, they moved me on back to the public school into the seventh grade when I was still at the 5th grade level. My first report card in the public school was four D's and one F. I remember my sister went nuts yelling, "Are you stupid or something?" Well, years later I realize, I had completely missed 6th grade altogether. I remember thinking, "Why am I so dumb?" Nobody else in my class needs help reading." My sibling used to scream at me at the kitchen table to "sound it out." I remember crying out loud, afraid to read out loud because I could not sound the words out. All she did was yell and drill me until I would break down in tears. Then I would get yelled at for crying. Too bad I didn't know then that about five to ten percent of American children are diagnosed as dyslexic. I wish I could have told my sibling that this problem occurs in kids who are bright and verbally articulate, but who struggle with reading. I wish I could have told her that Einstein was dyslexic and no one called him "dumb."

No, I just had to live with the very helpless feeling trying so hard to accomplish something that I just mentally could not do. Then, having someone I feared screaming at me for hours (so it seemed) and for all the candy in the world, was just the icing on the cake. I could not sound out the words, and I caught he** for it!

I have always hated reading out loud, and have never told my counselor this story. It's funny because I have been reading this whole book to her—chapter by chapter—for close to a year now. I am about two-thirds of the way done and look forward to reading to her every chance I get.

DANNY'S BIRTHDAY PARTY

In sixth and seventh grade, I was the only girl who was allowed to play with the boys. No other girls were allowed. I don't think the boys considered me a girl, and they definitely respected me like one of their own. There was the head of the group and his name was Paul. I was considered his "girlfriend," and we led the group at recess. Another student named Danny was having a birthday party, which I was invited to until his mom stepped in and said that no girls were allowed to go to his party. That was the first time in my life I can remember I was not happy being a girl. I was devastated to think I could not come to a birthday party because I did not have a weenie. *How dumb is that?* I thought. That devastated me, and for the first time, I felt like an outcast in my own group of friends.

FIGHTING BACK

I was in fifth grade and had gotten into a little fight with a male classmate named Ron. I guess I must have punched him a little too hard, because he told his high school sister about me. The next day she found me in the hallway and threatened me. OK, that was very scary for me. I mean, I was only in fifth grade and she towered over me like a parent would. Yelling at me, she told me to leave her little brother alone or she was going to beat me up. Well… I was not the one who started it. I was sticking up for another student when we had gotten into the fight.

I lost total respect for Ron as a boy. Remember, I was in a house with four boys, so I was taught not to be a tattletale or I would get beat up. Although she was intimidating, I was not going to just sit back and take it. 'So Ron can dish it out but can't take it,' I thought. In Helen's world, there was a price for that. I needed to pay him back for being such a baby. I told others of what he did by being a boy and having his big sister come down to threaten me, a girl. We teased him until he cried, and then we never bothered each other again. I know he looks like the victim here, but this was a bully who messed with the wrong little girl. In life we all must learn our boundaries. It just happened to be his turn.

OK, so maybe this one is not "abandonment," but I did feel all alone when his high school sister cornered me in the hallway. I really had no one to turn to other than myself. I was just in the point of my life where I was learning to fight back.

PUNCH MY BEST FRIEND

I have a friend named Karen in high school. We had been friends since sixth grade. When we were in high school, I ended up going to a party that was not far from my house.

I was to spend that night at Karen's house. I walked outside and heard Karen say something about me behind my back (so I thought). To this day, I do not remember what it was that got me so very angry, but I walked up to her and punched her right in the face. She took two steps backwards and fell on her butt. With the look of "What the h*ll did you do that for?" in her eyes. I yelled something at her and she yelled back. We stopped speaking to each other the rest of the night. For the first time, I felt betrayed and abandoned by my best friend. I had trusted her dearly. I am sure the alcohol didn't help anything. That night I ended up being too drunk to go back to my own house. So Karen and her friend Tony took me back to their town to decide what to do with me. Karen didn't want me to stay at her house, because she was still upset with me. No one else could take me home either.

Finally, Karen broke down and said, "She can stay with me." I may have felt abandoned by my friend, but the next morning I got a big shot of humble pie. Not only was I waking up at my ex-best friend's house, but I was sleeping in her bed. I rolled over to see where she was, and found her sleeping on the floor. I am sure you can imagine how 'feeling humbled' was an understatement! I promised her that I would never ever hit her again. In fact, I made a vow to myself to never do that again, and I am proud to say *I never have.*

She said, she was not even talking about me that night... oops!

When I bring this up, she always says, "She shouldn't have worn cowboy boots, that is why she fell down," and I always laugh and say, " Yah, yah I just knocked you on your *ss, just admit it." She laughs and says, "No, it was the boots."

Karen (Critter) is still my very best friend today!

CLASS GANG UP

OK this one caught me by surprise. One of my teachers thought it would be a fun exercise, I guess, to have the class give me spankings on my birthday... Do you remember how much I love people knowing it is my birthday? Not. Well, she told them, which infuriated me to start with, then thought it was a good idea to have them try and spank me. This did not go over very well with me at all. In fact it was quite a lonely feeling, mixed with abandonment and betrayal. I must admit, I threw a couple hard punches, and pushed a few of them back pretty hard, as my survival mode had kicked in and my adrenaline was pumping. I guess I was not getting the warm fuzzy feeling she thought I would, and she noticed this was not going over so well. She finally had them stop before someone got hurt. It was not going to be me; I was not one of the people laughing, thinking it was funny. I guess your average student would have welcomed the attention, and I know she meant well.

I guess it's another realistic look at how my past affected my future. Don't corner a wild cat!

THE ONLY STUDENT WITHOUT

After high school I attended a Bible School. I am not the smartest when it comes to books, and not only did I have a hard time reading, but I also had a hard time remembering things. My first semester cost me a lot of poor grades. I got better as time went on but in the end, I did not get enough points to get my paper showing I graduated. I didn't know this until the day before graduation. So I invited my sister who raised me to the graduation ceremony. Thank God she couldn't make it. Every single person I went to school with walked down that aisle but me. Two whole years of my life, and I have no paper to show I was even there. Although it was not a college-affiliated school, it still was a devastation to me.

MY OWN TEAM

This one broke my spirit. You can read the whole story in the chapter entitled *Football*. I owned and managed a Women's Pro-Tackle Football Team for five years. My head coach sabotaged our future by loosing games and getting our players to forfeit the remainder of our final season. Some players called our league and told them I was mishandling THEIR money. The league told them I was not doing anything out of the ordinary that any other team out there was doing. This team was everything to me. We put so much money and time into it. It really blind sided me when it all went down. I could not watch football on TV or talk about it for almost two years. I still don't have the interest that I used to. How can something I built actually end up betraying me? I would still like that question answered.

Some of them wanted to start their own team, but none of them had the cash to get it started. I shut the team down for good, vowing NEVER to go back.

MY STORE

I found a store that Pat and I just loved to go into. I felt like I was on vacation every time I opened the doors and walked in! It was filled with nautical and tropical decor. After three or four months, the owner told me he was selling it and wanted me to buy it because he knew how much I loved it. I was beside myself. WOW! I would love to own this.

I trusted this man like my own father, the one I really never had. He was a very nice Greek man with one of those moustaches and happy faces that make you smile when he does. We got along so well, and he made me feel so safe. How could I say "no?" He would take care of me in all this, I was sure. Well, little did I know, he was a con artist and thief. Money was his god. To make a long story short, he took me to the cleaners. I was left high and dry, without a second thought. I was devastated to see that one person could be so crooked and still claim to baptize children. Abandonment is just one of the many feelings I walked away with.

I rest in knowing my God is a Just God!

MY ONLY CHILD

You can read more in the chapter entitled *My Son*. I saved this entry for last for a reason. It is very, very personal to me. In fact I am a little hesitant to say too much because it's so personal. I have one child, a son who I love more than life itself, who has not spoken to me in over seven years. This one cuts deeper than all of the above abandonments put together.

In fact, I had to give this one to God, because it was just so heavy. I simply could not carry it any more. I cry when I think about this for more than 20 seconds, and an unbelievable amount of pain floods my heart. It hurts to the point where I could drop to my knees in sorrow. I do not truly know what I have done to hurt him so deeply, but I do know how time is so very precious and how every day that goes by is one day that we will NEVER be able to get back.

"There is no pain like the present, and no true relief within... BUT My God!"

37

MEETING LITTLE HELEN

This has been so therapeutic for me

I told my counselor, "I remember when I was younger, one of my abusers would give me things after he violated me." I then told her, "I am wondering if that is why I don't like to receive gifts?"

I also recall when I was married, my husband buying me a dozen roses and me responding with, "You can't buy me." Guess what? He never bought me roses again. I believe that was my Little Helen, trying to sabotage my relationship with my husband. She (Little Helen) doesn't think she deserves those beautiful roses. So I say something hurtful to stop him from treating me that way. This is all part of the dysfunction in my head, part of the sickness, but you see that identifying and admitting it is also part of the fix. It is the first step in healing and growing to become a mentally healthy person in the long run.

First, I realized I had a problem, by questioning myself. I asked myself "Why?" Why did I say that? What did I expect to get out of it?" You see when I ask myself these questions, I am forced to think about the situation from my adult viewpoint. My child who is still alive and running wild in me, she is the culprit here. She doesn't think rationally she just does without thinking. My adult has to go around picking up her mess and straightening up the situation. By doing this, it forces Little Helen to grow up, because I begin to really understand how she works. Eventually, I started to learn how to intercept Little Helen's actions, because I learned why she was doing it. I have found out that most of the time it is her low self-esteem that is causing the outbursts of negativity she displays.

To be honest with you, it was my husband (at the time) who told me I needed to find a counselor to help me with my anger problems, and our marriage that was falling apart. It's the best thing I have ever done for myself, in so many ways. When I found out there was such a thing as a Little Helen, I must admit, I did not love her. In fact—part of me actually despised her. I guess because Little Helen brought back so much of the past. These are things I just didn't want to deal with or think about. I think when I realized how out of control my life was, I was forced to stop and ask *why?*

I am going to reveal the actual letters I wrote to Little Helen to help you see what I went through. This has been so therapeutic for me. I can't believe it myself. Mind you, it helps a lot to have a good counselor as well. I explain more about that in chapter, Finding a Good Counselor. By sharing my actual letters with you, I'm guessing some people will think this very scary, but if I can help just one person, it will be so worth it to me. I know in revealing or not, NO one can hurt me any more, unless I let them, and you can bet your bottom dollar, I won't be allowing that.

My first real counselor, Linda, gave me an assignment of some questions (some with many parts). I noticed that I never did answer all the questions, But I will share with you the ones I did, and will answer today the ones I didn't.

Workbook

PART II

This can be used as a self-help book for you too, by answering the questions below.

As you are reading this today, I want you to know, I am NOT the same person I was at that time. I have grown to be confident and have no fears (OK, maybe spiders!) I don't even fear death—in fact, I welcome it. That may sound morbid, but I mean it in a good way. I can't wait to be face to face with My Jesus.

1. WHAT HAPPENED TO ME?

3/19/91

As a child, at about five-years old, I was sexually assaulted and abused by an older boy. I told one of the boys I knew and trusted about what had happened to me. I hoped that he would support and protect me, but they did the opposite. He and another boy sexually assaulted me, just as the first one had. That was horrible, but it only got worse. A man who lived with us sexually abused me, which went on for years. How many years? I really don't know. All I know is that I was a very scared, lonely, and confused little girl. Because of that, I have a low self- esteem. It's nothing short of a miracle that I could even function. I was destroyed.

I don't really let others see my low self-esteem, but it's there. I believe that being a Christian has really helped me with my self worth. Knowing that, some day I shall be higher than the angels. Before God, sin free and knowing if I were the only person on earth, HE would have still died for me alone. Now if that don't build self worth, there is nothing that will. These feelings of strength really solidify the fact that there is a God and that he is a wonder.

When I wrote this, the scary part was the reality of it going on paper, it now becomes very REAL! Not a comforting feeling by any means.

I never said this was easy... it's NOT! I struggle inside myself constantly, but again that is how I've grown from making mistakes to learning from them. We all learn things everyday, so why not make ourselves well by doing it?

155

2. HOW AM I AFFECTED, BY WHAT HAPPENED TO ME?
7/16/09

I am going to answer this question now, because I never answered it back in 1991 when I got the assignment.

- I am very cautious of people who I don't know, and I'm always on guard.
- I tend to scan parking lots or any room when entering.
- I sit with my back against the wall in most rooms.
- The blinds must be shut in a lighted room at night.
- I put a privacy fence up in any backyard I have ever owned.
- I check all the doors in the house before I go to bed, even if someone checked them before me, I must check them myself.
- I prefer to be the last one in the house, to make sure all entered safely.
- When out at social places like bars or restaurants, I am on guard, constantly monitoring where everyone I know is and what is going on.

One of my abusers used to try and peek through the bathroom door keyhole when I was going to the bathroom. Little did he know, I could see the shadow of his feet at the bottom of the door. I believe that is why at night I must have the blinds shut. I don't like the fact that others can see me and I cannot see them.

• **Self worth** - I don't know if I would've been a Christian today, if I hadn't gone through what I did in life. My self-worth today is because I believe Jesus; he has made me priceless to God and I'm aware that the devil has a deep-seeded hate for me.

• **Relationships** - I am an honest and very trustworthy friend to anyone. I have learned to respect others. At a very young age, I was betrayed by those who supposedly loved me. I truly know what REAL love is, but only through Christ my Savior. My counselor wants me to add the word MEN to relationships. I think I could write another book on that one. "How am I still affected by what happened to me in regards to:

• **Men** - I know I can't live with one and be truly happy (right now). I don't respect them equally like I respect women. I truly believe they are a weaker species mentally. When it comes to physical control, they have very little control without Christ in their lives.

• **Sexually** - I have never lived a life with no sexual abuse or exposure since I was five-years old. There was a time in my life (likely because of all the abuse) that I was a bit of a sex addict. Today, I am much healthier and not at all a "sex addict." I have vowed myself to God, unless I am to marry.

• **Strengths** - I am a survivor, NO death, no man, or spirit scares me.

• **Pain** - No one can hurt me unless I LET them, I control my pain level now.

3. HOW HAVE I COPED WITH SEXUAL ABUSE?

THEN—3/6/91

Well, to the best of my knowledge, back then I tried to avoid my feelings in order to cope with having been abused. I know I isolated myself in my room a lot! Maybe that was my way of punishing myself—or perhaps protecting myself. Maybe by hiding away from people, I felt that I wouldn't have to deal with my sadness and shame. I blamed myself for a lot that went on in my life.

If I had a problem with a friend, I usually felt that it was my fault. I also remember burning myself with a red-hot safety pin. My "self" was so numb that I really don't remember feeling the pain. I almost felt better after it was done. I also remember hitting many walls, once fracturing my knuckles. This would only happen when getting into a fight with someone. The harder I hit, the more pain and the better I would feel. The time I fractured my knuckles, I was almost proud of it, like I had accomplished something. No pain no gain...?

I look back and can see the sickness in my childhood. I can remember the feelings and the pain I felt inside me. A very lonely place I once lived in, I don't feel that unthinkable despair today. But—I do remember all these memories vividly. I believe the chains that bind us are those that we allow and control. As an innocent child—NO. But as an adult—ABSOLUTELY!

We each possess the power inside (and through Christ) to control our future. I just chose to face mine and make myself well.

4. HOW DO I COPE WITH SEXUAL ABUSE?

NOW-

Oh, boy. I don't know. By going to counseling, I guess. I'm coping so much better now, but many times I had rages of anger, mood swings, and lengthy arguments with my husband. For all the things that would make me unhappy, I took martial arts so I don't and won't put up with feeling vulnerable again. I would prefer death!

Well, I started writing this back in 1991 and had just started my counseling sessions, Linda. I liked her a lot, and as you can see, she makes me work at finding myself. I am not one of those who finds a counselor to waste their time by lying about myself or not telling the whole story. I do my best to tell all, ugly and painful as it is to talk about. All the details of my past come out as poison, and are replaced as water for growth. If we choose to leave the problems of our past buried, they will eventually fester and catch up with us. We will go on to say and do things that we cannot control. These are called temper tantrums, addictions, and self-mutilations which some of you probably have already experienced—not a warm fuzzy feeling at all. Growing is not easy, but it's well worth the effort!

TEMPER TANTRUMS

I am going to touch briefly on the subject of temper tantrums.

Temper tantrums are the anger that you, the adult, are NOT controlling and acting out because your little child did not get his/her way. One of the things I did to help myself at the time of a temper tantrum coming on, was count to ten before I reacted.

We are survivors and I know for me, the anger got so real and powerful, I could have killed, and I don't say that lightly. Just being totally honest here.

When we reach the point of raging anger, we actually fear ourselves… right? Let's be honest. Exhibiting a bad temper is not a good quality and is not looked upon admirably.

Temper tantrums are undisciplined behavior in its purest form. It really doesn't help you grow to make yourself well.

Know that the more you start to understand your little child, the more you will be able to control your little child. As adults, we have learned that life does not ALWAYS hand us roses. But the little child within us is undisciplined and may not be aware of this. It is YOUR job as the adult to start the discipline process. Do not let your little child get away with fits of anger or anything that resembles a "spoiled brat." Like a parent, nip it in the bud, and teach yourself what is acceptable and what is not.

Understanding how to discipline your little child does not come overnight. Control of your undisciplined self will take time and most likely a lifetime. But little by little, day by day, and you will start to change for the better. Know that when you are in a heated argument, your little child is present. Front and center! Identify with that, and get him/her to BACK DOWN and behave! You need to understand that your little child does not rationalize… he/she just reacts.

It's your job to teach and discipline.

Take your pride and put it aside or you will always lose this battle.
It takes humility to win this job of self-discipline, and ONLY your ADULT has the power to win this battle.

Prayer is also a BIG help in learning discipline, and it's also possible that lack of self restraint could be a generational curse, if you grew up in a home where adults showed little self-control. Being a cycle breaker/leader is the right thing to do.

1. WRITE ABOUT LITTLE HELEN-

3/6/91

Little Neleh is very lonely, but she wishes people would just leave her alone.
Why can't they just leave her alone?!?!
She never hurt anyone, so why are they doing this to her?
It's so unfair!
She is afraid to come out of her room.
He (abuser) might be sneaking around somewhere.
What gives him the right?
Why must she live in fear all the time?
Why must she always have to worry where he is, or what he is doing?
She is very angry at him, she wishes he were dead!
He had no right!
NONE!

She was born alone, she will die alone, so what gives him the f*ckin right!
Just leave her alone! She doesn't need him, she doesn't want him; she hates him. She
wants nothing to do with him, she doesn't even want to see him or touch him, or know
anything about him. She hates the thought of him. If he were here she would spit in his
ugly face. If she ever found out he was hurting someone else, she will kill him. And it
(wouldn't) won't bother her one little bit. It's just one less, d*ck she'll have to worry
about.
P.S. If you see him, tell him his day is coming!

You probably noticed I wrote my name backwards which actually was a sub-
conscious act. I used to write my name backwards when I was in Kindergarten.
I can put myself so into my thoughts as a child, that when I let myself feel little
Helen's feelings, I think like her again. It just came out like that when I was writing, and I left it just like that.

A lot of anger, just poison, is pouring out. It's all GOOD! Again, it's better on
paper than in real life. I read this and remember the helpless feelings, the anger
and the pain, so much pain. I do not feel that today. Now it is only memories.
It's like a cut. You feel the pain at the time, then it scabs, then there's a scar. No
more pain, but the scar is still there. It becomes a part of you, not always easy
to look at, and believe me I know. I try to look at the bright side, you may ask,
what bright side?

Believe me there ALWAYS is a bright side, you just have to find it. How about,
Thank GOD that's not happening to me anymore side?

This is the very first letter to my little self: it took me three days to complete. Not
an easy assignment, but it became a lifeline to restoring my future. A lot of tears
and downright wailing have come from all this and it was very painful (at the
time). But in the end, it gave me a renewed sense of being as if a ton of bricks
were taken off of me.

No more secrets, guilt and shame... I found FREEDOM!

Each one of these numbered questions needs to be written down in your note-book and answered by you. I am showing these as examples.

2. WRITE TO LITTLE HELEN

3/10/91
Wow, What do I say? Hi, Helen!
I don't know what to say—you've been
though a lot. I feel like the big sister
that was never there to help you. But
I can promise you one thing. I'll never
let it happen to you again. You are safe!
You're all I got and I am going to help
you get better. You will someday feel as
safe as I do. I need you to get better.
You're a part of me. I know I couldn't
help you back then, but I know I
can now and I will, you'll see!
Hang in there my friend we're going to
See this through. I Promise!

                              -Your Big sister

I read these words today and can clearly see how far I/she has come. It's truly amazing. According to the dates on my paper, it took me at least three days to write that little bit. That first letter was not easy for me to write. It actually was scary at first, but then I got to the point where I couldn't wait to write again. In my past, there was A LOT of anger, which will show itself in my next few writings. Please know that this is O.K. This anger is like a poison inside me. I had to get it out, and better to do it in words than in actions. I have grown to learn how to control my anger. I learned how and also why it's there. *How can you fix something if you don't know where it's broken?*

Letters I have written to Little Helen.

Dear Helen,
I just want to write and let you know, I'm still here. I haven't forgotten you—you're not alone, I am here. I know you are very confused right now, as well as scared. You're also feeling guilt and shame, but please don't. You're not alone in this; lots of people have gone through and done as you. Be strong, face it, stand up and walk on. You don't need to look back right now, but you do need to face it. It only means growth.

I'm here, I always will be. I need you to be strong, please try!! Together we are going to make it, but only together.

Come Monday, you and I are going to overcome this thing and move on, promise me.

I know I am ready but I need your help.
Remember together,
YBS

3. WHAT HAS BEEN TAKEN FROM ME?

Again, I am going to answer this now, because I never answered it back then.
My inner peace and lack of shame

4. WHAT HAVE I LOST?

My innocence as a child,
My self-esteem,
The healthy way one normally thinks.

5. WHAT HAS BEEN DESTROYED?

My carefree, fun loving, childhood memories.
My son's relationship with me?
Believe it all stems back to my past somehow.

6. ANGER LETTERS

I wrote four Angry letters.
I wrote these venting my anger to those who have abused me.
I will not be putting them in this book, because they are full of cuss words and very personal.

I will tell you my guidelines in writing them—there were NO guidelines. I let myself go with these letters, I mean every word whether cuss word or not, I let it ALL out. Until, I could not come up with any more. I knew my abusers would never see these letters and it gave me the freedom to let it ALL out.
Everything I was feeling to everything I was thinking was written on that paper, and I do mean everything.

7. REAL LETTERS TO GIVE (If I choose)

These letters are the ones that got delivered, well three out of four did.

By venting with the angry letters, it gave me the ability to write these letters with a little more level headedness. I did not feel the anger towards the men who abused me like I used to because I had already spewed it out. So this was just a focus of, *I want you to know how you have hurt me.*

Two of the letters I mailed out.
One of them I have made amends with.
The other one I have never had any contact with, to this day.
Getting these letters sent does not matter to me anymore.

The third letter I delivered personally and then took the letter with me before I left the house.

Why did I take the letter with me? Because I knew if I had left it, it would have been shown to someone else. The discussion was between me and that person, who abused me, and I wanted to keep it that way.

The Fourth One, I never delivered.
I guess I just didn't care enough about him to want to go there.

I want to explain something before you read any further.
These letters are **REAL!**
I'm being totally open and honest with you the reader and I'm not withholding ANYTHING. If you think this is easy… **TRY IT.**

I STILL occasionally fight my carnal woman inside, but I know in order for you to understand or get it, you need an example. So with that being said, I bear my soul to you… out of love, compassion and obedience to Christ. I would NOT be able to heal any other way.

These writings are very intimate, and NEVER did I EVER think they would someday be put in print for a book for ALL THE WORLD to see.

I live for Christ and Christ alone, this life is no longer mine but His…. **I submit ALL of me.**

These letters expose my little child's sickness and confusion of what she thinks love is. In writing to her, I try to make her see her mistakes and wrong feelings toward a beloved friend.

I can't express in words how humbling it is to expose these letters to you the reader. But I stand sure footed and humbly before you.

MORE LETTERS TO LITTLE HELEN

11:00 p.m. Nov. 14, 1993

Dear Little Helen,

I know life was not so good for you, and to tell you the truth I feel bad for not really liking you, because you are a part of me. A part I don't like to deal with, and yet a part that is badly hurt and confused. I guess I feel it's time this distance between you and I stops!

You've got to be a very strong person or you wouldn't be here today. You are OK! And I'm going to help you through this if it's the last thing I do. We are going to make it together. I need you as much as you need me. Hold on to me! Your pain is remembered and felt by me, so you are not alone! Please don't forget that! I can't tell you I love you yet (although I want to), but for now it's just not true.

But the day will come. Please don't give up! We do need each other, don't forget that! I will teach you how to love and trust again. But remember one thing, *You cannot expect a rainbow without any rain.* It's not going to be easy for us. But there is a light at the end.

Talk to you later!
Helen

2:45 p.m. 11/15/93

Dear Little Helen,

Well, I learned more about you today—you are quite complex, I must say, but I feel good about this counseling thing. Once again, I feel we are growing closer together. I feel ready and eager to learn about you, a little cautious of the unknown, and maybe a little afraid. I think it will all be OK.

Please prepare yourself for much growth because it will take place. We need to spend more time with each other as time goes by. It maybe a little each day, I don't know. I know the more time I spend with you, the faster we BOTH will grow. I am ready for a growing spurt, how about you?

Kiddo, I need you to try and open up, I know it's going to be hard and scary, but it's got to happen if you want to grow up, and I know you do. Look at me. I love life; God made a lot of beautiful things and people. You need to learn to enjoy them. You're wasting time and living with unnecessary pain. It can go away, we can make it stop, but you must open up. I'm not going to hurt you. I am a part of you. You have nothing to be afraid of with me. I'm going to write you a poem because I think you need something special just for you!

I love you !!
Me

First time I was able to tell my little self I loved her

TAKE MY HAND

Take my hand little girl,
And walk with me.
I know of a place,
Where the sun meets the sea.
Can't you see little girl,
I feel the pain you do.
There is no one else that knows,
Exactly what you went through.
I'm a part of you,
You are a part of me.
Don't throw your heart,
Into the sea.
Take my hand little girl,
And walk with me.
Hold with all your might,
For I can set you free.
Walk with me,
Talk with me,
Laugh with me
Open yourself up,
To what it can be.
I want to love you
Hold you, know you
Please won't you let it be?
Take my hand little girl.

-Helen On Wheelz –11/15/93

11/13/93

Dear Little Helen.
I felt as thou I was missing something in my day, so I decided to write you before work. I guess I was feeling "empty." I am finding a peace when I write to you.

Something I have never felt before. I don't know for sure, but I think it's good.

Well, we made it through another day, or the start of one anyway. To be honest with you, this counselor thing has been on my mind a lot. I am feeling empty about life right now but don't worry, I am under control of the situation.
It's just a feeling !!

There is a lot going on with the business, that is taking a lot of my time. Just less time to think about confusing things, I guess?

All I know right now is I feel the need to spend more and more time with you. Half of my time in life right now, is spent on how to make you well.

This time we are going to make it, if I got to get you there all by myself. I mean it!! You are worth everything to me right now. I am becoming more and more intensely focused on you these past few days. My care and concern for you is growing along with it.
I know this is good. See, we are making progress!!

Well, gotta go make money,
Catch you later,
Me
P.S. Can you see the light yet?

11/14/93

Howdy Little Person,
It's me again, just want to say "Hi." We have another meeting tomorrow morning. I guess I just wanted to see where you are. My husband says, "We have been very mean to him since we have been going to the counselor." I guess, I know why you're acting up so much—it's because we are working with you. I can't say I like it, it's very hard on my marriage....to say the least. I know you are not too up on this counselor thing; you are being exposed, but what can I say?
It's got to be!

We're going to make it this time, no backing out! We're going 4 wheeling until we get to the end. So you better put your seat belt on and hang on, there is no stopping until we are
finished.

Love,
Helen

11/21/93

Dear Little Helen.
Well, I guess I am writing to let you know I am still here. I haven't forgotten about you. You're a very important part of my life. My future depends on you. I never thought of it that way, but it really is true. I know of your ways, I just want you to know that!!
I have noticed you can be a sneaky little sh*t but it is ok, I will help you grow out of it. I guess I noticed it because I am not that way. I want you to know I really don't like that part of you, I hope it stops!! PLEASE work on it !! But really, I

think it's my fault because I allow it to come out. Better yet, we will work on it !!

Well, gotta go,
Catch you later,
Me

Allowing or exposing these letters in this book is beyond humbling. It's like opening up your diary to the world. These letters reveal my Little Helen's sexual attraction to my best friend. Yes, she (Karen) has given me permission to expose this. It is not easy, but how can you (the reader) see the real truth if I do not share it?

Dear Little Helen,
Well, I think it is time you and I face the real facts. You and I both know what THAT is. But I am going to write it out anyway to make it reality. Well, it became reality tonight. I am not afraid of it. I guess I am cautious. Yet, at the same time I am glad she knows. You see, I feel the problem between you and I comes down to the word **LOVE!**
Really what is love?
Do you really know?
I don't think you do!!
To you love is sex....why?
Because it feels good?
It's all you know.
That's how love was shown to you.
People can show love and affection without sex.
It doesn't have to be touching someone, or pleasing someone in a physical way. Love can be expressed in words, or a simple hug or kiss. The touch of hands, it doesn't have to continue with sex or a physical pleaser.
God loves us—no sex is involved.
God's love is greater than ANY love. God loves us with an agape love. This love lasts forever and lasts through anything. Because of this love, even though she knows you will never win. Your love is a selfish love just like the one they used on you, when you were abused.
Can you see the comparisons?
She depends on us. We are her friend even if she were to pursue it, we could never let it happen. Think of the consequences, the kids, our relationship with God and our relationship with each other. God's love is not selfish, it thinks of others first!
You MUST REMEMBER that!
Your selfish thoughts are wrong!
Think of the many years of faithfulness as friends. Don't let her down, she deserves better. If your love is real and true you will know better than to let her down in this way.
I know you have these wrong feelings for her and I understand them, but I don't agree.
Feelings are not always right, don't live by your feelings, it is The Word of God

166

that is true. Follow it. It won't steer you wrong and you won't regret it!
The Bible tells us to be Christ like, our love for Him should ALWAYS come first!
It's true, everlasting and it's right!

You are a strong person. Don't give into cheap imitations. Just like I tell my son, "Be a leader, not a follower." Now that her and I both know what is going on with you, I don't have to be afraid of you anymore. You have been found out, I feel this is good, it's OK. Now we can deal with it. You're not alone. Don't feel embarrassed It's a part of you. Remember, I know her like the back of my hand, she knew about this along time ago. She is not stupid and neither are you!

I am just glad it's out, no more hiding. NOW, we can start dealing with the problem.

Yes, I love her dearly but I will only allow you to give her an unconditional love. She is the Best and deserves the best. Don't ever settle for second. You need to learn REAL love, not cheap imitations.

Let me put it this way:
Say you did have a sexual relationship with her?
Do you think it would last...?
Would it grow to something really beautiful?
Or would the guilt and shame destroy the beauty you have now?

We both have kids, is that something we want them to grow up with?
Is it right?
Would our relationship with God grow stronger?
Who do you love more: God or His creation?
We need to keep our priorities straight!
Remember love is not skin deep!

I Love You,
Helen

12/5/93

Dear Little Helen,
Howdy Kiddo, it's been a few days since I wrote you. I've been really busy. The last letter was pretty long. I guess I felt we both needed a rest. I really don't have anything specific to write about. I guess the last letter was pretty heavy. You know that was a big step for us. To make it reality like that, but I think we all took it well. I think she might be calling tonight, we'll see. I miss her a lot, she is a great person. My problem with her is, I need to get her to stop looking up to me so much. I know what she is going through, I have been there myself. The thing is you really get hurt when you take that person off the pedestal. I got her wrapped around my finger and her and I both know it. It's almost scary!

My flesh loves it but my spirit is shunning. As her friend, I feel it's wrong but it's not like I asked to be put so high, she put me there! I guess, I feel as her friend,

I need to help her take me down because it's not right. If I think of it, I put her up there too. I don't think quite so high, not like God. She is a beautiful person, with a great personality and a heart of gold. I just wish you didn't come into the picture because it distorts the picture and makes it dirty to me. I know for a fact, if it wasn't for God and His spirit in me, you and I would get along just fine. I know her and I would be driving cross-country in a big old semi truck diggin' life to the fullest. But you know what? Our time on earth is like a drop in the bucket. The time we spend on earth would be in vain.

Kiddo, you may be a problem that I must deal with all my life and you may have your occasional shots in life but I know one thing that's true, you will never win in the end!!

I guess I finally have accepted you for the first time, for what you really are. You may feel angry at me for all this, but that's O.K.

I love you anyway,
Helen

I wrote her a poem

WHERE RAINBOWS END

> We have been friends for 15 years,
> Had lots of good times and a few tears.
> You call me Buddy, I call you Friend,
> This is one friendship, that'll never end.
> When my heart hurts, you feel the pain.
> When you have a storm, I can sense rain.
> Like 2 peas in a pod, we'll always be,
> Best of Friends, till eternity.
> There is no mile to far, or ocean too wide,
> To put an end to the love, we hold inside.
> Sisters we are and that will Always be,
> I treasure you like a pearl, I found at sea.
> As God is My Father and first love of my life,
> My hope to you friend, is to never bring you strife.
> Yet I am only human and you trust in me,
> You need to give credit, were credit should be.
> I know rainbows can flow, like an ocean wide,
> But you can't get caught in the colors inside.
> I will Always love and my colors will Always bend,
> Yet I am only human, so this is were rainbows end.

-Helen On Wheelz 11/28/93

12/25/93

Hey Little One,

Well it's me again, it's Christmas Day, and my best Buddy is here. Can you believe it? I still can't! Boy, this is the best present I could have ever received.

Anyway, how are you? You know I love you!! You don't scare me like you use to and you don't seem so dirty to me. I'm not so insecure about you. I guess it comes down to, "I'm not afraid of you anymore."
You are what you are....a child. I am what I am...an adult.
We will grow to become one!!
With me (the adult) leading the way!!
Just remember, I love you and I won't steer you wrong. People can say what they want, I am not afraid anymore and you shouldn't be either.
Take my hand little girl!!
Talk to you later,
Love ya,
Me

12/26/93

Dear Little Helen.
"Hi!" Well, it's out completely, no hiding anything now.
She knows everything and you know what?
I feel WONDERFUL!!
You should too, she loves us anyway!!
You don't have to be afraid, you are accepted for who you are but not for your wrong thinking.

My friend, come out of it!
You have it all, come out of it!
Take a look at what you have, the love I have for her is real.
Don't you want a part of it?
You will eventually see it my way. You will see this love is REAL and the best. You will slowly come around to all of this. I have never been so close to her in all my life,
It's a high! Intimacy, does not have to be sexual!
I love her like a sister and before God we are!!
This love is pure and beautiful.
I have the honor to be closer to her than anyone on earth without sex involved.
I wouldn't give that up for a cheap imitation—one that could end and feel dirty.
TRUE Friends NEVER say "Good Bye."
Lovers DO!!
Think about it.
Love Ya,
Helen

1/23/94

Hi Little Helen,

Well, it's been about a month since I have written. I have been busy, I guess? I feel you've come a VERY long way, these past few months. I think you are well over half the way through this. We need to start working on liking you.

Do you like you....?

Touchy question, I know.

Well, I need to tell you that I really like you.

I will tell you why you are a very strong person:

You don't need others to follow, you are a leader.

That's a very good quality!

You're sensitive to others and considerate.

You're outgoing and a fun person.

You are stubborn (that can be used for good).

You have a good and peppy personality.

You're all in all a winner!

I see you changing, getting stronger, becoming happier with yourself.

We're almost through with this... hang on.

It's ok to like you—you're a great person!

NONE of it was your fault!!

DON'T FORGET THAT!

Love you Always,

Helen

I didn't love myself when I first wrote these letters, but as time went on, I grew.

Little Helen, was a very confused little girl, because of the early sexual abuse in her life. Her social skills were tainted to say the least. This would be why so many who have been sexually abused at an early age become prostitutes. These letters are the honest and untainted though the process I went through convincing my little self that love is NOT sex. This is most true—especially when it comes to a treasured friend.

The one thing I was NOT aware of where the demonic spirits that were oppressing me at the time continued to stir. Little Helen STILL craved the sexual desires of being with a woman. That did not go away.

38

FLASHBACKS

MY GOD… HELP ME!

Flashbacks can be a very ugly word to some people. I know it was to me.
Some of you may not know what I am talking about. I am being VERY REAL in
this chapter and it contains adult content.

YOU HAVE BEEN WARNED!

My very first flashback is when I was two or three years of age and I was in a crib
crying because I was not wanting to take a nap. I was hot and sweaty, wearing
a one-piece fuzzy red pajama suit. Crying as if my life depended upon it, and
believe me, I thought it did. I couldn't speak a lot of words being so young, but I
can remember the outrageous anger, frustration, and gut wrenching loneliness I
was feeling. I was so hot my hair was wet and sticking to my forehead. My skin
was on fire as tears ran down my face soaking my neck and chest area. I remember feeling so alone as my family in unison laughs and says, "Cry a little louder,
we can't hear you." I understood their words and it made me even more upset.
I am holding the crib bars as I am jumping up and down as hard as I possibly
can. They are laughing at me… ALL OF THEM. I can hear them discussing my
behavior and laughing again and again. As if I am NOT a member of their family, but some worthless piece of trash they enjoy mentally tormenting. My world
is over, I hate that I am even breathing at this very moment, Just let me die". My
screaming grows louder and louder in frustration. They just keep laughing. Every time I scream at the top of my lungs, I can hear them all laughing and talking
among themselves. I know they are talking about me, but I cannot understand
what they are saying. I get the laughing, and it breaks my heart. My throat is so
raw from screaming I think I am going to throw up. I am more than upset; I am
down right heart broken.

I am crying as I am writing this at 50 years old. It is SO REAL to me. I had never
dealt with these feelings before or thought about this situation for more than a
minute or two.

What I am doing right now is taking myself back to think about my feelings as
a little child, and trying to remember all the emotions from that time. Actually

sometimes the memories become so vivid to me that all my senses come back. I sometimes can remember all the tastes, touch, smells, pain, and whatever I was going through at that moment. Looking back is often very painful but so very therapeutic. I believe this is why people have crutches because they can be used to block themselves from going back to deal with memories and pain. Once you are able to revisit your memories, what I call DEALING WITH IT, you start to heal.

Healing will not come until you deal with some unpleasant things first. I not only sometimes cry, I have downright wailed. This is all the (what I call) poisons or toxins coming out. I let myself feel the pain and cry for as long as I need to. This can feel VERY lonely and unbelievably painful but can also feel so rewarding at the end. I personally send up a quick prayer for God to protect and help me when I explore my past. I am in a VERY vulnerable state of mind and the pain of old experiences can be overwhelming.

There have been times that I have texted my counselor or a friend (as an anchor or life line as I'm walking through this hell), but usually when I write, I prefer to be alone. This particular time I texted my counselor and my friend Kathy from church.

This is the secret to HOW I have grown to be free of my past. I have learned to deal with my past, and I don't allow it to deal with me. If I see a problem, I fix it. There are times it has taken me years to fix a problem, but it's game on once I see it, and I don't stop until done. I do not dance around the mountain. I go through it.

As Pastor Patty said yesterday in our ladies group, "God wants us to be learning and continually growing—not complacent in life."

What have I done to cause my family to hate me?
Are they even my family?
Is this the purpose of my existence?
If so, why?
Why am I here?
I don't want be here… anymore!
PLEASE, take me from this miserable place!
I don't know what death is; all I know is, I want to stop breathing.
I want my head to stop pounding.
I want my hot and wet pajamas off of me.
I want them to stop laughing and making fun of me.
Can't they understand I need help?
Do they even care?
I am so thirsty!!
Can someone please tell me?
Why am I breathing?"
What have I done to deserve this abandonment and torture?
Why do you all laugh at me?
I am so thirsty!

172

This is my very first memory of my childhood at 2 or 3 years old.
But this next flash back is even worse.

Hang on Houston we are about to crash land!

This next flashback was so devastating to me that it did not resurface until 43 years of age. I am 50 now. When I tell you this is a life long journey, it REALLY is. This is by far the hardest chapter I have ever written but God for some reason wants me to tell it and I am obedient to His will. This is very humiliating to me but I am 100% sold out to Him, obedient & humble… no matter what!!

This is very graphic and dramatic and NOT meant for anyone who has not been sexually molested.

I believe I am in kindergarten or first grade at this time when right before bed someone in my family whispers to me to come into their room when it gets dark. I do not understand or want to do what they are asking me to do, so I ignore it. The lights go out, and I start to fall asleep. When I hear this person whisper "Helen, Helen" from inside my doorway. I open my eyes and my heart starts to beat so loud. It's dark time and I cannot see but I know who it is. I become frozen and do not say a word. They walk over to my bed and shake me, "Helen, wake up. Come with me, come over to my bed". I am confused, I say "it's dark time…. I can't." He takes my hand and says, "Come with me." As he pulls me out of my bed and into his room and into his bed. I am so confused… I'm thinking, *why am I here? I've never done this before.* I am so scared, it's dark time. He then gets into his bed and opens his covers for me to get in next to him. He then takes my hand and puts it on his leg (at least that is what I think it is). So I leave it there motionless, he then puts his hand on my hand and makes my hand move up and down on his leg. I am so confused, *why is he making me do this to his leg?* Then something weird happens, he has a little leg and it starts to move. My mind does not understand what is happening. He then takes my hand and puts it in his pajama pants and I am touching something soft but wiggly, something I have never felt before and I don't know what it is. He then lifts his whole body and pulls his pants down to his feet. His little leg is sticking up in the air. *I don't want to be here or touch this leg thing… what is it?*

MY GOD… HELP ME!

I am crying so hard, the pain and unbelievable betrayal and confusion. I can so vividly feel Little Helen's every emotion and pain like it's happening right now, all over again. How did I ever make it through such a sick experience?
I can't believe I lived through this. So much PAIN!!!!

He then takes my head and pushes it down near his leg and his leg hits me in the face. I have no words, I am so confused at what he is trying to do to me. He then tells me to "lick it." My mind is dumbfounded, *what? Why would I want to lick your leg?* But he says, it again, "Lick it." This time in a very stern voice and pushed my head against it. I smell a musty, pungent odor as I open my mouth and do as he says. I begin to lick his leg when I hear him make some kind of low groaning sound. Then in the same stern voice he says, "suck it" again, I do as he says as he pushed my head down on to his leg. He then again makes a low groaning sound and tells me "yes." *Whatever that means, I really don't care. I just don't understand or want to be here doing whatever it is I am doing.* My mouth is getting very tired when I taste this salty kind of slimy stuff. It comes out of his leg. I am so confused. Then he makes a louder groaning sound and lifts his hips off the bed and this warm kind of salty, slimy stuff comes out of his leg. I spit it out of my mouth and pull away. I just don't understand, *why he pottied in my mouth, so that little leg is where his potty comes from? I get it but why would he want to potty in my mouth?* I do not get that !!! What just happened I do not seriously understand at all, *why would he potty in my mouth? Why?* I am so confused when he flips me over on my back and pulls my pajama bottoms down to my feet. I say, "what are you doing?" He says, very sternly, "sssshhhh!" I am so scared and confused with all this. I close my eyes and pretend I am not even there. I can feel him climb over me he is very heavy. Both of his knees are on the outside of my body as I feel his hard little leg push on my butt, I mean the place I go potty from. I think we all go potty from there, don't we? Why does he want to touch something that dirty comes out of? He pushes hard against me, I feel this unbelievable sharp pain go shooting through my body. I immediately start to cry and he tells me to "be quiet." So I start to cry louder from the pain I am bearing and don't care if he says, "be quiet!" I am NOT going to be quiet. So I let out a wail of a cry, and he stops pushing completely. He seems angry with me, he pulls up my pajama pants and tells me to go back to my bed. In my mind I am so confused, *is he mad at me for not letting him hurt me without crying about it?* I think, *GOOD!* I jump out of his bed and run back to my room. This never happened again, that I can remember.

As an adult looking back today, I have no anger towards him. I do not fear him or hold any ill feelings towards him. In fact to this person I say, " I forgive you." I believe we have the power in our minds and through Christ (only) to control how much people effect our future. Those I trust and love, I give the right to affect me emotionally. Those that have hurt me or betrayed me, I DO NOT. My choice!

You have betrayed a child of God and God's Word says in:

Psalms 35:1
"Contend Oh Lord with those that content with me;
Fight against those that fight against me"

I am protected by My Heavenly Father !!

The past is exactly that... the past. I cannot go back and change it but I can change my future and I choose to NOT let this situation affect my future anymore... PERIOD!

I am not running from this or feel any emotions anymore from this part of my past. It's called **my past** for a reason. It's why the rear view mirror is so small and the windshield is so big.

174

I was feeling a whole lot of emotions as I was writing or preparing to write this flashback. It fact, I fought with God for over six weeks before I started writing this one. I did not want to write this experience out on paper. I cannot emphasize enough but every time I turned around someone was speaking about giving it ALL up for Christ and not sparing anything. How we should confess all and be free. I can go on and on. Until finally, I actually got out of fellowship with my God because I was angry. He wanted me to tell ALL. My flesh/pride felt very humiliated or humbled by telling this story. With many tears and a confused heart, week after week, struggling NOT to give in. I finally asked my friend Kathy from church, out of desperation "why, why must we tell all?" She was walking out the door in front of me, she spun around and said, "because it can help others."

Again tears filled my eyes and I knew these were God's words to me. I cried out "LORD, WHY, WHY MUST I GIVE ALL?" HE said to me, "did I not give ALL?" That was enough for me... as I am totally humbled.

This is the most personal thing I have ever put on paper, my flesh and my pride hate this chapter BUT this book is NOT for me... it's for YOU the reader. I am finding the closer I get to God, the less of me I am needing to please. The odd part is; I am free of those chains that once bound me. Those crutches that controlled me. Those fears that held me.

I have given my life to The Lord COMPLETELY, not 99.5%... ALL of it! HE ALONE is my ROCK, I believe in The Holy Bible and read it daily.

I am rock solid in my faith and Heir to the throne of The King Of (ALL) Kings. I want for nothing in life but to help others find the Peace I live in daily. I have told this only to get you to understand. YOU too can be Victorious in life. It only takes you wanting it bad enough.

Do you?

Draw near to Christ ONLY!! He can heal your past and free you from the bondage satan wants us all to live in. In fact satan hates that I am free from my past.

To him I say, "YOU LOSE AGAIN!

I am Victorious thru Christ Jesus. His shed blood was enough and many others will be free, in Jesus Name.

39

FORGIVE AND RESPECT YOURSELF

Learn from your mistakes and grow.

Forgive and Respect yourself. I can't say that enough. You have got to know that what happened to you as a child **WAS NOT YOUR FAULT**!
Do you understand that?

Please, stop right now… close your eyes and repeat those words,
IT WAS NOT MY FAULT!!
IT WAS NOT MY FAULT!!
IT WAS NOT MY FAULT!!

I want you to mean it with all your heart and soul and mind and to BELIEVE IT! Because it is the truth!

You were A CHILD!

You were NOT an adult, and technically your parents or guardians were responsible for you and your actions—just like mine should have been.

A reality check looks at my relative who had the audacity to bring a child molester into our house. The sick part of it all is that I remember her arguing with him about the way he looked at me.

Can you believe, she was actually jealous of me… a child?

You see, lots of times the people who are at fault may not be very stable themselves. People who are not stable tend to attract people who are not stable. (Birds of a feather flock together.) It's sad, but many times the children end up suffering from the results of their instability.

I am a victim of unstable relatives and their "friends." As messed up as my childhood was, I refuse to allow this dysfunction to ruin my life. It was NOT MY FAULT and I refuse to take the blame. I was a VICTIM, BUT CHOSE TO BE A SURVIVOR!

This is probably the most important thing you need to understand. Survival mind-set is the first step toward building a solid foundation of growth and self-worth.

FORGIVE YOURSELF
RESPECT YOURSELF FIRST
FOREMOST... YOU ARE NOT TO BLAME!!

As children, we grow up thinking that because we are the kids, our parents or adults don't make mistakes, and it must be the child's fault. Well, I am here to tell you, that is not true in all cases. I am a mother as well, and I have made many mistakes. Your little child thinks like a little child and will believe that anything negative that happenes is all his/her fault.

It's your responsibility as an adult to change that thought pattern.
YOU (the adult) are in control now and must teach your inner child the truth, and the truth is: You or your inner child are not to blame, never were and are not now. As the adult you must believe it first, or you will never convince your little child that this is true. Just like I did, talk yourself through it, and believe it. I told you it was my sibling who brought the child molester into our house.

Did I lie? No, that is a fact. She did allow him to move into our house. I had no say in that matter, and neither did I have any say when he came up to my room at night when my relative was not home. She was my guardian, the one the courts made responsible for me. She was not responsible for me only when she was home or only when she felt like it. She was responsible for me at ALL time until I graduated from high school.

What happened to me as a child is a result of poor decisions to expose me to a very sick man, who was sexually aroused by little girls. I was forced to live in the same house as this mentally sick man, and I was repeatedly exposed to his sick ways.

Is any of this my fault? I think not, and I refuse to allow their horrible decisions to destroy my life. And... it is exactly that... MY LIFE!

I and only I, have the power to deal with what happened until I can see them as totally powerless in my life.

Now it is your turn. Talk to yourself, and prove to yourself that anything bad that happened was not your little child's fault.

Why? Because it wasn't!! It's humanly impossible for the blame to justly be placed on ANY child's shoulders. We were children and were certainly not responsible for adult's actions.

If you did things you are not proud of as a child, remember they were taught to you by someone else. Children tend to copycat things that they have seen or have had done to them.

177

This is a normal reaction in a child's behavior. You were no different than any other child.

You know what? I too, have done things I am not proud of in my childhood... so what? I did not know better then, but I do now, and so do you. I am no longer doing them and you shouldn't be either. If that is the case—then you are on the right track.

Forgive yourself for your past mistakes, stop beating yourself up; you were, and still are, human, we all make mistakes. Learn from your mistakes and grow to be a better and stronger person because of them. That way, the mistakes we have made are not made in vain.

Ask God to forgive you for your past mistakes or wrongful doings. Then let them go because God no longer remembers them... only we do.

When He died on that cross for ours sins, He was not messing around. He meant it with EVERYTHING He had. Our wrongdoings are gone from His memory once we ask for forgiveness.

Psalms 103:12
"As far as the east is from the west, so far has He removed our transgressions for us."

Remember, mistakes are not wrong as long as we learn from them.
Now forgive yourself and move on.

40

BULLYING

It's TAUGHT or LEARNED

So you may be thinking, was I bullied in school, too? That's got to be why I am writing about this topic.

You can't be farther from the truth.

I WAS the bully.

I first want to say, I am by no means the same person I once was. Not only has my God renewed my mind but I am very opposite of who I once was in elementary school. What exactly was I? Well, I was full of:
• Anger
• Hate
• Evil thoughts
• Lots of inner pain
• Deep-seated guilt
and I wanted REVENGE! On someone... ANYONE!

We all want to point the finger at the one who is acting out as a bully.
We need to understand!

That bully is a bully because, he or she has been bullied by someone else. In most cases, this is not a personal trait that we are just born with. It's TAUGHT or LEARNED from something that influenced the bully.

Go back and look for the source and you will solve the whole problem from beginning to end of **why the bully is acting out** as a bully.

Sick (in the head) people are raising children every day. We need to STOP blaming the victims of these sick people; they are just copycats of real problems they see only too often.

These are **bully children** who have learned from the examples of adults. They are impressionable otherwise innocent kids who were badly corrupted.

I have put this sentence in another chapter because it is so true. **We make mistakes (over and over again) because we have not learned how not to.** When a child is being abused, victimized and/or mistreated, it may be ALL they know how to be. This was their life's lesson.

Stew on that for a while.

Sin passes from generation to generation.

Exodus 34:7
"Keeping steadfast love for thousands, forgiving iniquity and transgression and sin, but who will by no means clear the guilty, visiting the iniquity of the fathers on the children and the children's children, to the third and fourth generation."

41

FOR MEN ONLY

Your opinions depend on how you grew up.

I realize by the title, woman will be reading, too ;-)

I am 44 years old as I am writing this. I am not claiming to know anything except for my very own experiences and because of that, they have become my personal beliefs.

You may agree with some of the points I make, and may not agree with others. If you don't agree, that is perfectly fine—you have a right to be wrong... just kidding! No, seriously I am just writing about a few things that I have learned along the way in life.

I have thought about a certain topic for a long time, and fought with myself about whether or not to even put it in this book. My final decision is to state my mind about this subject because---well, because life is just too short. The subject is: MEN.

I have been accepted in many circles of boys and men in my life from grade school to the present. When you guys talk about your girlfriends, mistresses, ex's, baby mommas, sisters, and moms, I have heard the good things you say about girls and women, and the bad. I've heard how you respect some of them totally and others not so much. I've listened to the true "I love you" feelings toward some, and others none at all. It seems to me that most of you think relatively in the same manner, but yet a lot of your opinions depend on how you grew up and who raised you.

Just like us women, our past experiences truly influence our future behaviors. So in a lot of ways we are a lot alike, but the one thing that sticks out to me is, "We definitely do not process things alike."

I believe the roles of men and women in this life are meant to be different, but men are clearly not embracing their roles as spiritual leaders as is stated in the Bible. Their lack of leadership is causing a great devastation toward the future of mankind. Many don't even see this.

Let me explain: If you believe in the Bible, then you believe that God made man. And if you remember, God made Adam and the animals, but in doing so, Adam was not happy. When God made animals, they were created so that they all had a mate. God realized that Adam was alone and needed more. So God took one of Adam's ribs and made woman or Eve.

If you believe this is a true historical happening, then it makes sense that you should truly believe that woman was made for man... right?

Conversely, it is clear that "God did not make man for woman." Do you believe that? If you are following me, then you should be able to see that it truly means that we (women) do not need men... not like they need us!

Then this is where the problem is setting in for us as a human race living in a free country.

Years ago, man was the protector and the provider, and woman truly needed man's help. Today, because of technology and civilization as it is,
we (women) have proven through the course of time, to be able to make it on our own if need be. Look at all the single mothers raising their children alone. Women surely prove it here.

Man is failing to do his part in the very place God intended him to be strong—at the head of the household.

Some women have been forced to take on the entire load of basically "doing it all" by themselves. Alone. It seems that nine times out of ten, when a man leaves his woman, (often with children to care for), he goes on to find himself another what? Yes, another WOMAN! And on it goes...

Now, the first woman is left to fend for herself and her children, and she must fight to the best of her ability to raise them alone. Many times, the woman is not interested in finding another man after being severely hurt by the first one or two. It's a sad picture, but the number of damaged women in our world has caused a shift in what God intended for us. Not only are children being raised without fathers, but women are remaining mate-less. Many women do not care to return to a married life.

If they do find someone, they often choose to live out of wedlock.

If you are one of these women, please don't ever think for one second that you don't matter. We all matter and affect each other every day, whether it be positive or negative!

How do I know this?

I am a mother who left my husband and son to carry on with my own desires. Do you think it mattered to my husband or son that I left them?

Well, let's see. Neither one speak to me. They both want NOTHING to do with me... so what do you think?

Did I matter to them?

There are many men who actually think that they are irresistible to us women—like we literally can't live without you or something. Like we totally depend on you. Well, it's time to wake up and smell the roses.

It is actually the opposite
Here are some of the reasons I say this:

1. How many Ladies clubs are out there, with male strippers?
2. How many Gigolos do you see walking down Main Street?
3. How many ladies just can't take it any more and must rape a guy?
4. Who sells more magazines, Playboy or Playgirl?
5. Why are there free drinks for the ladies at the clubs?
6. Why are our T.V. commercials laced with sexual innuendos and female models?
7. Why don't women think of all these sexual ideas and bother co-workers sexually?
8. Why is it mostly our businessmen who are aggressive to others?

Take the strip clubs for example I would bet 90+% of them are owned by men. In fact, I just read a statistic from an actual woman strip club owner who said that there are "only two or three other women owners in the United States." She agreed that the women who dance in strip clubs are often girls who are struggling in life with no family support to rely on. Many of them have higher hopes for their lives and need money to escape the life they are in. So... basically women have a need to dance in strip clubs, and that need is money. If there weren't a need, the clubs wouldn't exist at all. We all want to blame the stripper or the hooker, but it's the man's weakness that is causing this need to exist in the first place. I mean, really? Is it normal to run wild in a nightclub and take your clothes off? Is that really OK? I don't think so!

There is a reason for all these differences of men and women. Man needs woman more than woman needs man. I am just being straight up honest here. I hope that if you are man reading this, you will read on with an open mind. I've got to tell you a secret about all those ladies you see who are all dressed up when they go out on the town. I know that guys think they dress up for them, but it's not the truth. We really dress up for each other. Now don't get me wrong. There is that innate God-given drive in us to mate, but it is nowhere nearly as strong as the drive that men have. I know that God put some "drive" in all of us to keep humans from extinction.

To all the men--
God has put YOU at the head of the household.
He has put YOU as our leaders.

A lot of you are not leading.

Many of you don't know how to lead.

You often walk away from God.

You want to live on your own, without God.

You are failing miserably on your own without Him.

Women are seeing your failures more and more clearly. Women are starting to walk away from YOU.

Devastation is bound to be the end result of men failing.

We as a civilization CANNOT make it without God leading our men.

I truly believe a man without God is only half a man.

A very large percentage of men are extremely weak regarding anger and morals.

Modern day man tends to lack in commitment and leadership.

Someday I will see God and I will have one important question to ask Him: *Why should I (or any woman) allow a man to control my household when he can't even control himself?*

It makes it very difficult for a woman to choose a mate when he has nothing to offer her in the end other than divorce and a few kids she must raise on her own. Statistics show that "Daddy" will decide to start his life over again with another younger woman.

Are you kidding me?

Today's women are getting the 'let's wait and see' attitude toward having children. I just read two articles pertaining to how women in their childbearing years are refraining from having children. *They are allowing their jobs or studies to take priority in their lives. I can't help but think that we (as women) are getting smarter and wiser by not allowing history to repeat itself.* What's happening is women are starting to wait and see how their relationship goes for a few years before they are even thinking about having children. With contraception available, it's wise for women to wait awhile to be sure that their relationship will live on before they find themselves getting stuck alone with kids and no husband as a support. In the long run, absentee parenting will only cause devastation to our population.

Thousands/millions of women are waiting to see what is going to happen in their relationships to focus on their careers first. Then it seems to me that thousands of babies who would be born are not going to have the chance until mom feels safe enough in her relationship to allow it to happen two or three years later and let's not even throw in abortion rates.

If the relationship works out and she feels she is ready. She starts to bear children, the problem is that the first or second child she was supposed to have, never got born and never will. That's when the thousands start to turn into hundreds of thousands before too long, and we are in deep trouble through the course of time. I can't help but think it already may be too late. This is a domino effect of not having our men as leaders. We as women need to have men in our lives in order to feel safe and secure to produce our future generations.

You may be thinking to yourself, *how can I be putting all the blame on men?* In a sense I am, because you must understand that is how God views it. YOU (man) were put here first to lead us and provide for us, to care for us and protect us. God has put men at the head of the household. YOU are the ones who must answer to Him first and foremost. We were put here to be your helper or helpmate not to lead you. God has given YOU the power to allow us to make life. Yes, we bear life but not without you. YOU are the first one to choose who is to receive YOUR seed or not, and if she is interested in you, you win her love. A majority of YOU just give it out freely and don't care who she is. You don't take the time to even get to know her name much less anything else, because it's just a one-night stand anyway. Where is your pride and honor in choosing if she is even good enough for you or your off spring? But you see… there isn't any pride. You are there to satisfy yourself in this… not her, and so you can justify your behavior in doing so. This is why we have the one-night stands, date rape, pornography, (and for some of you, it goes deeper into child molestation, child-pornography, bestiality, rape and others but I will get into some of that later in this chapter).

Listen to me very carefully… *God is alive and well and so is the devil you need to choose who is to be your leader. You are not free to walk the line, if you choose none, then you have chosen the latter, and you will walk without God and destruction shall be your offspring's outcome. If you want to be a leader, then you must let HIM lead you and your offspring will be blessed by YOUR decision for generations to come.*

I wrote this for all the men who don't have God in their lives. Just because your mommy or daddy did not raise you to believe there is a God is NO excuse when you meet Him face to face… and YOU WILL!

I wrote this because you do matter. God loves you so much. He died for you, so don't take Him lightly. Because He didn't take you lightly... He gave His ALL for YOU.

YOU GOT TO MAN UP

God has put YOU in charge of your household,
It's YOU who stands before Him answering for your fold.
The sins of our Fathers are spinning 360°
We're headed for destruction, can't you see?

Man, you got to man up before it's too late,
The circle of life is crashing at your gate.

Our prison cells are filled with you,
12 to every one woman…it's true.
You're in for addition, affliction, rape and murder.
Your Momma raised you, you got no Father.

Man, you got to man up before it's too late,

The circle of life is crashing at your gate.

You want a woman, but you can't hold true,
To the promise you made before your honeymoon.
So you leave your girl...for what?.... Another,
Yet you can't support the seed from the other.

Man, you got to man up before it's too late,
The circle of life is crashing at your gate.

She's getting wiser, she's getting smart,
She don't need your lack of support.
Why settle down and buy a home,
When in 3 to 5 she'll end up alone.

Man, you got to man up before it's too late,
The circle of life is crashing at your gate.

-Helen On Wheelz

Be responsible as an adult, as a man, to seek him yourself. He is not dead just because you ignore Him. Life goes on, but some day we all must die and on THAT day it will simply be too late for excuses.

We as a civilization simply cannot make it without God leading our men.

My Counselor thinks I am a little harsh in my writing about men, but she understands where I am coming from. She seems to think I hate men. That is not true. It's the respect for men that I am having a problem with. A lot of men I have been exposed to in my childhood have seemed weak to me. Their biggest weakness appears to be their attitudes toward the opposite sex. I have observed men as they sit in the lunchroom at work, watching just about every woman who comes in the door. I was talking to a friend of mine as I saw one particular man staring at a lady and said to him, "You know she sees you—right?" He said, "What?" I said, "She sees you looking at her." "No she doesn't. She didn't even turn her head or her eyes when I looked at her." I said, "You know we women have peripheral vision, too." He started laughing and said, "Yeah, I guess."

They say men have the capability of undressing women with their eyes. I asked a few guy friends that question and all of them said, "Yes they do." "So really—what does that mean?" He simply said, "I can see her naked in my mind." I said, "Really, is that why full-grown men like cartoons?" He started laughing and said, "What?" I said, "I used to like cartoons as a child but as an adult, unless I have a child in the room, I think they are a waste of my time. But men seem to still love them. I am guessing because you all have big imaginations that it makes it easy for you to see women naked when they aren't. I don't know of any women who visualize men naked, at least not that I have heard of. I guess we could if we really tried, but most women don't focus on that when they first meet someone. I think there are other things more important to us than just physical looks in a guy, like his personality and his heart—you know, emotional things. We are more interested in his character and most things that matter outside of the bedroom. Most women want a man to make them feel safe, secure, and grounded in life. The sex part would be just that… sex. Of course, sex can also be another way of expressing love, if the relationship is of equal opportunity! Sometimes a woman just wants sex and nothing more, but most of the time, I think women are in relationships for much more than just sex. We are very emotional creatures by nature and tend to look to the future.

There are increasing numbers of men and woman coming from abused homes, so there are more and more people wanting something that deviates from being conventional in the relationship department these days. So now you have today's average woman not wanting to get married at all or waiting much longer to feel safe enough to bear children. The divorce rate is over 50% in the first three to seven years of marriage.

What is happening to our society?

"God's eyes are never closed," is a quote from my friend, Dr. C. Becker. Just because our T.V. and media have desensitized us by selling everything from candy bars to drug prescriptions using sexual innuendos, does not mean we are exempt from the consequences. We are and will continue to pay dearly and more severely as time goes on. We have become a weak people.

God has put man in charge of the household for a reason, and it is not to be taken lightly. The problem I see, is a majority of our men are NOT being led by God. In fact, many are not even leaders, themselves. They follow the latest trends or find themselves stuck in imaginary toys like video games. The latest gadgets have captured their utmost attention. They can barely cook to feed themselves, and without microwaves, boxed foods, and restaurants, I truly believe the average single man would have to live close to mommy.

Maybe I am a little harsh?
I guess I want to know what happened to THE REAL MEN? The one who knows how to humble himself: He knows how to raise his children with proper discipline.
He has better self-control over his own eyes and mind.
He knows what the words "Cherish and Respect" mean.
He knows right from wrong, and can hold true to correctness.
He knows how to love unconditionally.
He respects his elders as well as authority.
He can control his own temper.
He knows the word "Sacred."
He can hold a real job.
He loves his Jesus.
He reads the Bible.

He is a leader.
He is honest.
He can cry.
He gives.
He...

This SHOULD go without saying but I am going to say it anyway because it needs to be said...

He pulls up his pants because he is... A MAN!

WHERE WE BELONG

I was confronted the other day,
"Why have women turned out this way?"
"What do you mean?" I asked the man
He put down his paper, and said with demand.
"You all want your rights, you all want what's fair,
But when God created man, you women were not there!"
Man came first can't you all see,
If it weren't for our rib, you would not be!"
"This is a true statement, one I believe,
But don't be so boastful that you can't conceive.
There is a real answer to your mystery,
If you give me a minute, I can help you see.
We were not started from man's mere toe,
To be trampled on when he goes to and fro.
Nor were we created from a mere hair off his head,
To be worshipped as Goddess, the 1st commandment said
We were created from mans side, to be his friend,
Not to be treated as a 2nd class citizen.
To walk behind you is an insult to our making,
To walk in front of you would be wrong for the taking.
Put away your pride and boastful song,
Allow us to walk beside you, it's were we belong"

-Helen On Wheelz 1996

42

MIND FREAK

The devil loves to mess with our minds.

10/16/17

I have got to talk about the mind before I finish this book... it's the devil's playground. I titled this chapter Mind Freak for one reason: "The devil loves to mess with our minds." It's where he gets his greatest victories. His biggest battles are won in OUR minds and he knows it. Our thoughts happen to be the weakest area in our lives. He likes to control us though our minds and thoughts. When we react to the unholy thoughts that go through our minds, He becomes victorious.

You see, our mind's focus becomes our destiny. It's where we are going. Our FOCUS is our EVERYTHING! If I have your focus... I have you.

I want to give you an example in my own life. I usually listen to praise or Christian music because it is 'safe' for me because my mind stays focused on God, Jesus, and The Holy Spirit. If I change it up and start listening to country or modern secular music, I have noticed that my mind starts to shift. There is a whole lot of talk about sex in those lyrics. Guess what happens to my focus, my actions, and my control?

I lose it. What happened to Peter when he took his focus off of Jesus while he was walking on the water? His mind shifted to the height of the waves and the water began splashing on his face. He lost his focus and became consumed by his situation. Do you see this story is actually our own lives? We live THAT situation every day. The waves are the problems in our lives; where is our focus? Are they on Jesus or the world? What are we filling our minds with daily? What are we consuming our brain waves with? Who/what is occupying our thoughts?

Have you ever heard these sayings?
"Garbage in, garbage out?"
"You are what you eat."
(They are true statements for the mind as well.)
It's NOT just the music we listen to. It's everything that fills our day:
The people we hang around with.
The T.V./Movies shows we watch.

The video games we play.
The internet we expose ourselves to.
The books we read.
It's EVERYTHING that consumes us.
Everything that we think about takes up space in our minds. Are they Holy? Are they glorifying to God? We all want God's help but are we willing to help ourselves? Are we? Are you willing to renew your mind?
Because THAT is what it will take for us to win this battle in beating satan.

Let me ask you...
Is the pain of your past unbearable?
Are you depressed?
Do you feel lost?
Do you feel worthless?
Do you hate yourself?
Do you hear bad voices in your head?
Do you feel lonely?
Do you hold hate in your heart?
Do you worry all the time?
Do you desire the wrong things?
Do you like to feel physical pain?
Do you watch porn and can't stop?
Do you desire to be with the same sex?
Do you take/do things to harm your body?
Do you wish you could be faithful?
Do you live with guilt or shame?

I can go on and on and on, but I think you get the picture. If you can answer "YES" to ANY one of the above questions, then I am here to tell you, *You are right where satan wants you!*

He hates us and wants nothing good for us. He likes pain, confusion, lack of peace, and turmoil In fact chaos makes him laugh at us... and why not? He whole heartedly hates our guts.

I Peter 5:8
"Be self controlled and alert. Your enemy the devil prowls around like a roaring lion seeking someone to devour."

You see, if he can control our thoughts, he owns our actions too.
This is NOT something we can win over on our own because if we could, we would not be having the problem in the first place.

An un-renewed mind cannot please God; in fact it can't even hear God.

Colossians 3:2
"Set your mind on things that are above, not on things that are on the earth."

Romans 12:2
"Do not be conformed to this world but be transformed by the renewal of your mind, that by testing you may discern what is the will of God, what is good acceptable and perfect."

Romans 8:6
"For to set the mind on the flesh is death but to set the mind on the spirit is life and peace."

There are so many good verses I can't put them all in here. Do a Bible verse search on the word: Renew—it's amazing.

The devil wants your headspace. He will try to distract you any way he can—anyway he thinks he can get you to lose your focus in life. If he can, he will keep our lives and attention filled with temptations for things around us like Worldly Music, Video Games, T.V., Movies, Commercials, News, Internet, Sports, or the neighbor's husband/wife. He has our minds... hook, line, and sinker Hollywood, Disney, Soap Operas, the love of material things. Why does he need to show face? The worldly things already have ALL our time and mind space.

You want help?...
Are you ready to put some effort toward your problems?
In other words are you ready to man/woman up to discipline your mind to become the Warrior you're designed to be?
Are you ready to take responsibility for your own actions and renewing your mind?

If you answered "yes" and want help, then pray this little prayer:

"Heavenly Father, I come before you broken and full of sin.
I surrender my whole self to you.
Forgive me, Lord.
Take all my shortcomings and teach me your ways.
Open my eyes, my heart and my mind to your will, Lord.
Renew my mind to be obedient to you in all that I say and do.
Give me a brand new start in life and protect me.
Make me the Warrior for you that I am meant to be.
In Jesus Name,
I Pray, Amen"

If you just prayed this prayer sincerely,
I congratulate you for taking a stand.
God hears you and His will... will be done.

Take responsibility for your actions and be aware of what you expose yourself to. Protect yourself from everything that temps you to stray. Start throwing things out of your life, that are not Holy or positive... that includes people who are negative for your life.

This will take time, but little by little you will start to see who is for you and who is not. God is for you, but people who talk down to you are not. God loves you, but people who abuse you do not. God is always there for you, so draw near to Him and you will never be disappointed.

I did NOT say life is going to be roses because no one's life is. We learn and grow from hard times. But every time we stand tall after a fall or a lesson in life, we become victorious. Through Him, we become stronger.

YOU ARE A WARRIOR ! Don't ever let ANYONE tell you otherwise!

One more thing, if you begin to pay attention to HOW you are being attacked, you will start to notice a pattern. Satan is very cunning, but one thing I have noticed is his ways of temptation are always done in the same way. Once you learn his patterns, you will see that he is not so creative. He tries to trick us with the same thing over and over again. Learn his ways of attack, and you will win at his little games in your life. Once you've learned them and stop falling for them, he gets bored and goes away. But... DO NOT put your guard down, because stupid he is not! Keep your eyes focused on Jesus at all times, and read the Bible to learn His Word... this is our sword and protection. Mere words repeated from The Holy Bible will cause him to flee in most cases. He is not very big and bad if The Holy Spirit is your protector. You need to learn to use the authority given to you with your title of A Child of God!

Fight the good fight and know you are Victorious through Christ Jesus! Amen

43

CROSSING OVER

The word "CROSSING OVER" (I thought) usually refers to someone's spirit going from one place to another, once dead. But I stand corrected. When I asked Siri (My phone), this is what I got:

CROSSING OVER
NOUN The exchange of genes between homologous chromosomes, resulting in a mixture of parental characteristics on offspring.

This is NOT what I am talking about, what I am talking about is:
Crossing Over, from the worldly, carnal and devil ways of living to the Godly, Pure, and Holy. Where I have given Him (God, Jesus, Holy Spirit) full authority over myself including my whole life.

AM I perfect? No Way! But my heart is right with Him. and I seek His face daily to the point of desiring to give Him ALL of me... no matter what... even if it means death.

Philippians 1:21
For me to live is Christ and to die is gain

It took me 50 years to get to this point.

I finally gave in, in 2016 when The Lord told me to get baptized again. I say "again," because I was baptized as an infant (growing up Catholic) and then fully immersed in Bible school (non-Denominational). I was sitting in church when Pastor Joey told the congregation that they were going to be baptizing in two weeks.

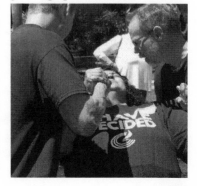

The Lord said to me, "You need to get baptized again." I remember being very confused, so I said, "What? I've been baptized twice already." He said, "Helen, this time it is different." So I called Pastor Kathy, the one in charge of Baptisms at our church. I explained to her my situation. She was so happy for me, and two weeks later I was both baptized and prayed over by three Godly women—Pastor Kathy, Dr. C. Becker, and Pastor Patty.

God has so Blessed me with a solid church foundation and character examples who have been there for me. I have said this before: It's good to surround yourself with people who you want to be like. If you want to be more like God, then hang around those who live in that manner. This can go both ways, positive and negative. It starts to feel like a chess game, where you set yourself up for your future moves. Shoot for better characters amongst you—meaning finding people who are more Godly than you. The best direction we should all focus on is forward learning, upward growth, and moving toward bettering ourselves.

Break yourself away from people who are swearing and cussing, and are still trapped in the worldly ways. I call these ways, the devil's candy, which is smoking and uncontrollable drinking… and more.

If they can't control the little things in their lives, you can be sure the big things are still in their closets. It doesn't mean they're bad people, they are just not good examples of what you want to copy.

I'm NOT judging them… God sees all. I'm Just trying to help you see the personal example of how I moved forward. Very few people actually get here, because very few desire to give God ALL of themselves. Many stay in the lukewarm zone, and only cry out when they need something. This is average and it is not where I wanted to be. I'm not saying I'm better than anyone because I certainly am not! I'm just saying—I'm willing to give ALL, and with that comes the benefits of living a life of peace and tranquility. It is the one think I could not find living as a lesbian because it separated me from my God. Any sin separates us from God… ANY sin, big or little. I have found that when I pray and read my Bible, and sin is still my friend, it will keep me separated from God. I can feel it in my soul, like He is not near me. I had lived this way for years as a lesbian: hot and cold with God.

44

SHERRY'S SONGS

These are poems or songs that Sherry Baker has written and I wanted to share her gift with you and include them in this book to honor her. (Used with her permission.)

I CAN'T SEE THE SUN

I can feel the sun go down on me,
The breeze is blowing and the leaves are rustling free.
But I can't see the sun,
No, I can't see the sun.
I can feel the coolness of a fresh running spring,
I can hear the robins and the blue jays sing.
But I can't see the sun,
No, I can't see the sun.
I've walked this path so many times before,
I wandered aimlessly I can't find the door.
The mountains cry as if to hear my voice,
They know I'm lonely I've got no choice.
Cuz I can't see the sun
No, I can't see the sun.
Evening draws nye now
The air is getting cold,
I know there is darkness
For me it's all of old.
Cuz I can't see the sun,
No, I can't see the sun.
I've walked this path so many times before,
I've wandered it aimlessly I can't find the door.
There is a blindness more than you know,
First it takes your heart and then it takes your soul.
Cuz you can't see the sun,
No the only living Son.
I once was blinded but now I see,
There is so much more for both you and me.
You and me.

CHASING RAINBOWS

I can sense a feeling when you're far away,
You can make a mountain move by the thoughts you conveyed.
I can see your smiles die yet you keep on playing the game,
Don't you know it makes me cry to wonder why,
You keep chasing rainbows in the sunshine.
I know what you are feeling now,
You feel like there is nowhere to go.
Please remember me my friend
I'm here to help you grow.
There are many storms ahead,
They're there to make you strong.
But if they seem to make you bend,
I'm here to lean upon.
So don't go,
Chasing rainbows in the sunshine.

I WONDERED AIMLESSLY

I wondered aimlessly on the beaches of iniquity,
I cried, The Lord knows I cried.
And I wondered why was my heart so lonely,
Why didn't I know where I was going?
Why, why me?
Then one day The Lord came to me,
He said, "Child I died to set you free,
Then why are you ignoring me?
Then why are you running from me?'
I wondered aimlessly on the beaches of in iniquity,
I cried, The Lord knows I cried.
And I wondered why was my heart so lonely,
Why didn't I know where I was going?
Why, why me?
Then one day The Lord came again,
He said, "Child slow down I just want to be you're friend,
And take my hand and follow me and we will walk thru eternity."
I wondered aimlessly on the beaches of iniquity
and I cried, The Lord knows I cried.
But now I know why,
He told me why.

I DON'T LIKE TO PLAY GAMES

Sometimes, I think the world is playing games with me,
How can I play if I don't know the rules?
Sometimes I cry,
Sometimes I die,
Deep down inside.
I don't like to play games,
When lives are the pieces.
So please don't play games with me.
Sometimes, I think the world is playing games with me,
How can I play if I don't know the rules?
Sometimes I cry,
Sometimes I die,
Deep down inside.
I am your sister and I am your brother.
I am your friend,
Can't you see?
I don't like to play games when lives are the pieces,
So please don't play games with me.
Cuz, sometimes I cry,
Sometimes, I die deep down inside.
Deep down inside…mmm.

YOU'RE MY FRIEND

As I walked that path alone,
It seemed long and oh so narrow.
Many times I'd just stopped and cried
Oh, why must I walk it all alone.

But like a rainbow in a dark cloudy sky,
You've shown me colors that I've long disguised,
And in your gentleness you've proven to me.
You're a friend.

As I sit upon this rock and ponder I'm forced to ask of God.
What has brought me such happiness?
I just don't seem to deserve it.

But like a rainbow in a dark cloudy sky,
You've sown me colors that I've long disguised.
And in your gentleness you've proven to me,
You're a friend,
You're my friend

45

MY SON'S ANGELS

You almost got hit by that car.

Our son was only 4 years old when my husband had moved to Florida, trying to start a business. It was a very cold winter evening in January, and I just needed a few things from the store. I bundled my son up in his snowsuit and his winter boots, and we jumped in our car for a quick ride to town. The Sentry Store, where I liked to shop, was on the other end of town but it wasn't far. We lived in a pretty small town, so we were only seven to ten minutes away. I remember... it was a very cold evening and something just didn't feel right.

I was at the check out when My son said, "Mom, can I please have a quarter for the bubble gum machine"? I didn't have that many items on the conveyor, and the checkout lady was almost done. I searched in my pocket for a quarter, and when I handed it to him I said, "Hurry up, I am almost done here." He said, "O.K.", took the quarter, and ran over to the gum ball machines that were lined up at the front of the store. I remember I had a six-pack of soda in glass bottles and a paper bag that was half-full of items. My son was standing in front of all the machines trying to decide which machine to put his quarter in, when I walked past him and said, "Hurry up, I am leaving."

There was another couple walking in front of me who were wearing trench coats. They were tall, slender, and seemed so together and bonded within themselves. They stepped on the rubber mat that opened the sliding glass doors, and I followed right behind them. I tucked the half-full paper bag of groceries under my left arm that was holding the 6-pack of soda. The couple walked to the edge of the sidewalk and both stopped. I walked to the left of them and could hear my son's snow boots rapidly hitting the ground. I knew he was at a full run trying to catch up with me. At that very moment, I heard both of them yell in unison, "LOOK OUT, A CAR!" I could hear the sound of the car as it approached way too fast to be in a parking lot. I was looking straight ahead, so I did not see the car... or my son. There was no time to even turn my head to see, but I put my right hand out away from my body, hoping to catch my son before he could run ahead of me into the direct line of the speeding car. I caught him on the top of his chest, his momentum pushed my arm forward, and I tightened my fist around his snowsuit. His feet were lifted up off the ground and I set him down on the edge of the sidewalk as the car goes flying by. I looked down and said, "My God, you almost got hit by that car." I looked up to thank the two people in the trench coats for the warning, but suddenly realized that I was outside the store—alone with my son. Tears ran down my face, as I realized what had just happened.

This is just one more piece of proof to me that the spirit world does exist. If there are good spirits, you can bet your bottom dollar that the bad ones also exist. For whatever reason, The Good Lord chose to make my son's Angels appear to my human eye and offer their power of speech to come to our aid. I know for a fact—God spared my son's life that night.

BENEATH MY HEART

My son, my strong hold, my tranquility,
Beneath my heart you will always be.
Shining like a beacon, in the storm filled night,
Keeping me strong, on course and willing to fight.
You make my life, so worth while,
With your laughter, energy and beautiful smile.
May God always bless you with laughter and zeal,
That you may know John 3:16 is real.
People, places and things in life,
Can cause pain, confusion and strife.
Focus on joy, inner peace and agape love,
These are things found only above.
Life is a lesson so study it hard,
Always double check, and deal a straight card.
Stay true to yourself and know your heart,
Don't hold anger in, it will only tear you apart.
My son my strong hold, my tranquility,
Beneath my heart you will always be.
I Love you so,
Mom

-Helen On Wheelz/ January, 2000

50

TRUCKING

I gave up the love of my life for the One who gave up His life for me.

I graduated from "Trucking School" in the fall of 2012. At that point, my life was falling apart, or at least that's how it felt. My girlfriend and I were breaking up, and I was past the point of stopping it. I had introduced her to the guy who worked as my handyman, and their rela-tionship had begun. She and I got into a very heated argument—I mean, like never before. I so loved her, but the end was in sight and my inner child was raging and losing all control. I was crying uncontrollably and unbelievable anger was coursing through my veins. I was seeing "Red" and could lose it in a split second. One day I turned from her and punched my fist three times through the drywall in our bedroom. I just missed a two-by-four by a fraction of an inch. My world was caving in fast, and jealousy was my friend. Even though I knew I needed *out* of this relationship, letting go was not easy. I grieved tremendously, and I knew I had to run. So... I accepted an Over The Road Trucking job in Texas. I am never one to go backward in life, so running forward seemed only right. Moving on was one of the hardest things I have ever done in my life, but at the same time, it was really one of the most rewarding. I gave up the love of my life for the One who gave up His life for me. Sin separates us from God, and no matter how I tried to justify it, living with someone outside of God's blessing is never holy. I could pray and read His word all I wanted, but I could never break through to the one thing I craved within myself. I always thought it was sex—but I was so wrong. It was finding a real peace within myself. I had not really been living before. Peace was not my friend. I justified my actions and pretended to do the right things in life even though I knew in my heart and soul that peace was nowhere in sight. Before I did something that I would regret, I went ahead and jumped on a plane to Texas to run from my past. I didn't look back. I just focused on the future of myself as a truck driver. I studied and learned all that I could, and I did it as fast as possible. Before graduating and being certified to drive solo, each driver had to team up with a fellow student driver for three weeks. They gave us the name, "Dumb and Dumber!" My teammate was a student named Carol. The two of us went out on our own for over three weeks. Carol was a lot like me in many ways. Living with someone in the space of (basically) a closet was not easy, but Carol and I became very close. And yes, I cried a lot during those three weeks as I disclosed my past to her. In those days, Carol was the only person who made me feel like I was not alone in this world—besides God. She really helped me understand myself, which was a blessing from God for sure. Carol and I are still really good friends today. When we call each other on the phone, we always say we are, "Alive and Kicking!" And... even if people don't get us, "That's how we roll!"

TO MY FAVORITE SON

My Son, I am so sorry for the unfair world you were brought into.
For not showing you the love you so desperately needed to hear or feel.
For the dysfunction you were forced to live with.
For the loneliness I know I caused in your life.
For not being the mom I wanted to be to you.
For the countless words I said or didn't say.
For the arguing you were forced to hear.
For not having a stable home for you.
For not knowing how to.
For divorcing your father.
For not loving myself.
For leaving you.
There is not a day, I wish I could go back.

Knowing and Being what and who I am today:
Full of Life,
Full of Hope,
Full of Love,
Full of Jesus.

And YOU being who you are today?
A Marine,
A Husband,
A Father,
A Believer.

Even, if I never see your face on this earth, I know in my heart of hearts.
My love for you will only grow, and I will pray for you without ceasing.
YOU Hold My Legacy and YOU WILL BE BLESSED MY SON!

I Love YOU Like I love NO OTHER,

Sincerely and Forever,
Mom

RECOGNITION

Karen,

Thank you for being the crazy Critter who allowed me to experience high school life outside the building. You have always inspired me to play sports and to win with dignity, even if it meant beating the boys.

Thank you, for being able to keep secrets and sometimes, some of my deepest thoughts. Your leadership and strength have become an inspiration to me and I am so Honored and Blessed to call you, 'My Very Best Friend... even at age 50+.

You have always been there when I needed you and that has never changed.

I Love you and Treasure every moment we spend in life's journey. Thank you from the bottom of my heart."

P.S. I can't wait for us get to heaven with Terry–I hope we get to play ball up there. <3

Sherry,

I don't know if you will ever know the deep love and admiration I have for you? You are the one who led me to the Lord in High School. That one selfless act changed my WHOLE purpose of being.

You showed me that the light at the end of the tunnel... was NOT a train. You brought hope and unconditional love to my eyes, knowing when not to speak and at times just being there for me, giving me an escape from my hellish world I lived. Just knowing you REALLY cared, saved me from a world of drug abuse and addictions.

There Aren't Enough Words blew my mind. To think someone cared enough to take the time to think of me with so much thought and feeling. Living a childhood so dark and corrupt, you will always be the breath of fresh air given to me by My Heavenly Father.
Thank you for loving me unconditionally.

You've got a friend,
IRF
P.S. Through Christ... Lives will be changed! Mine was!

My Nice,

What a beautiful friend you are to me. I am so blessed to be called your 'special friend' even though it makes me laugh out loud. You are A Warrior!! Don't you ever forget that. I know you will finish strong!!

Love,
Naughty

P.S. "I will roll with you ANY DAY Harley or 18 Wheeler"

My Full Blooded,

I don't think I ever told you how much you mean to me. You mean the world to me and I would not be where I am today without you. Although we don't always see eye to eye, I want you to know I am inspired by your loving ways and kind heart. Thank you for being the Godly example I need. Also thank you for asking God for me to be born. There were days I held that against you but today I thank you with all my heart.

May God Bless OUR Journey Together,
Love,
Your Full Blooded

Susan

I am so blessed to call you my friend. Thank you for reaching out to me and introducing me to others just like me. A beautiful window was opened when I met you and your husband Frank (my long lost bro).
Thank you from the bottom of my heart for ALL your love and support. For believing in my journey and opening my eyes to 'The Sabbath.'

Love you both!!
Helen Back

204

Dr. C. Becker,

My mentor and my friend, Thank you for being the strong rock I needed when times got shaky.
Thank you for having the patience to wait for me to grow spiritually and knowing when the time was right to wake me up.
You are the example I needed to know, it is possible to walk upright and stand tall, even if no one was watching.
But "God's eyes are never closed"
Thank you for the countless phone calls, when I needed them most.
For always having my back and never wavering.
I am blessed to call you friend.
Talk to you later Doc,

Love,
H.O.W.

Pastor Kathy,
Thank you for the heart to heart talks and speaking words of wisdom to me, when I needed them most. For praying over me when going 'back out' was not in my plans.
Thank you, for the time we had.
You will always hold a place in my heart.

Love,
Helen

Theology Degrees:
Dr. C. Becker, Doctorate
Helen On Wheelz, Associates
Pastor Kathy, Masters

THANK YOU

Pat: For the undying Support & Sincerity through out the years.

Mona: For the guidance and safe place you became. For instilling it in my brain to write THIS book.

Momma: For ALWAYS having an ear for me & a safe place to vent.

Mom & Dad: For giving us the opportunity to say those words "Mom & Dad" in our life. For welcoming us in your home like we belong. We ♥ you!!

Ritter, Ritter & Tracy: For not losing touch, when life took a shift. I miss you!!

Silvia: My beloved sister in The Lord... FINALLY!! You're friendship is beautiful blessing to me.

Danni: For being our sister from another mister.

Kat: For taking me in when it wasn't convenient. LET'S RIDE!!

Carol: Thank you for choosing me to be you're 'dumb & dumber.' Your insight & coaching were a God given Blessing when I needed it most.

Maryjane & Guy: For the countless prayers

MJ: For having my back on this WHOLE thing & nailing the cover. YOU ROCK my friend.

Jane: For meeting for tea & crumpets & completing the mission with expertise.

The Syms: For being a Beautiful Family & will ALWAYS consider mine!!

My Michael: For getting me to see I am not the ONLY ONE. Your leadership is an inspiration & your humility inspires me.

Dudie: For all the childhood years of good times. I treasure the memories. Miss you!!

Gage: For being one of the Most Beautiful Blessings in my life. Stay right with God & grow to become "The Warrior" you were meant to be.

Jacob: Praying someday I will get to meet you.

MY LORD AND SAVIOR:

People say you have a sense of humor. I am beginning to see it.
My life has turned full circle.
What once controlled me,
I now control.
What once scared me,
I now make run.
What once made me cry,
I now cry tears of joy.
What once held me down,
I now hold in my hand.
What once was dark,
I now see The Light.
What once was dirty,
Has been washed clean.
What once brought shame,
I now see as Victory.
What once grieved my soul,
I now celebrate my life.
He tried so hard to keep me down & all I had to do is look around.
You were there Lord.
THANK YOU for ALWAYS being there!!!
Thank you for being the example.

> *Love Your Daughter,*
> *~Helen On Wheelz*

MEMORIALS

KrazeeRay,

My dear brother you are greatly missed by so many. I so wish I had finished this book 10 years ago, maybe you would still be here today.

We went through so much as kids, I know you felt alone in life... but you were NOT!!! It was the devils lies. The Bible says "revenge is mine" sayeth the Lord, this book is a hard kick in his teeth.

Chains will be broken and lives will be set free, In Jesus Name.
I broke through to the other side and there is Joy and REAL Peace.
I avenged your life with this book, you will be proud when I see you again.
I know God can NOT deny his own and you and I will meet again.
Rest easy bro...
Our REAL Father has got this!!!

I love you!!
Your Little Sis
(Helen On Wheelz)

Yoly,

My Dear Sister, You are missed so deeply.
My time with you was so short, who would've ever guessed it would have turned out, as it did?
None of us is promised tomorrow. The Bible says, "our time on earth is like a vapor..." I get it NOW!!!
I changed the name of the book, from what we discussed. It's rock solid, you would love it. I'm telling it ALL, no more secrets. I don't know if I'm super brave or just plum crazy but I'm about to find out. Life is too short to hold it all in. Your short life has taught me that much.

Besides it's time the devil pay his dues. Someone has to stand up for all the hurting & trauma filled people. He's about to get laid out, with God's Blessing. Fighting for the WINNING SIDE...
ITS A BEAUTIFUL THING!!!

Love you Always,
Your Little Sis

EPILOGUE

Today, my life is filled with peace. I am not haunted by my past; I have grown so close to my Lord by giving Him ALL of me. It took me 50 years to get here, but life is beautiful now—peace and tranquility are my friends.

For those of you who have experienced major trauma, I am here to tell you, there is REAL peace in surrendering to Jesus. We were not meant to walk this life alone.

This book is my real life's story in the most accurate way I can portray it as a non-professional writer. Thank you for reading about my journey. My wish is that you have found a bit of enlightenment from my story—enough to raise your arms up to the Lord.

FINAL THOUGHTS

Thank you for sharing my deepest thoughts, which I must say were very difficult for me to express. No child should ever have to experience such turmoil and uncertainty, but unfortunately many do. When we have been robbed of who we are, the end is most often misery. I spent a lifetime learning not to look at myself, but to look beyond myself. Finally, when I looked to the Lord, I knew I had found the solution!

I thought it might be fun to end this book with a quick glance at my week. My wish is to encourage my friends and readers to stay positive and embrace the Lord at all times. Today is July 14, 2019, and I am still trucking OTR, with my cat 'Animal'. I am presently in Pennsylvania headed to Maryland and Virginia to unload. I will be retiring from trucking once this book is completed. It has served its purpose to finance the publishing of this book, allow me time alone with God, so the world's distractions did not interfere. I have enjoyed my time out here for the most part, but I must move on with my life.

I have put **ALL** of me into this book the way the Lord has asked me to. I pray chains be broken and God's will be done in **all** the lives willing to fight the good fight.

You are a WARRIOR, don't you forget it!!!

Sincerely and Humbly in Him,
Helen On Wheelz

57520493R00125